my dearest
SISTER

my dearest
SISTER

A HEARTFELT GUIDE TO THE LOVE, FRIENDSHIP, AND LIFELONG BONDS OF SORORITY LIFE

MELANIE J. PELLOWSKI

Skyhorse Publishing

Skyhorse Publishing books may be purchased in bulk at special discounts for sales promotion, corporate gifts, fund-raising, or educational purposes. Special editions can also be created to specifications. For details, contact the Special Sales Department, Skyhorse Publishing, 307 West 36th Street, 11th Floor, New York, NY 10018 or info@skyhorsepublishing.com.

Skyhorse® and Skyhorse Publishing® are registered trademarks of Skyhorse Publishing, Inc.®, a Delaware corporation.

Visit our website at www.skyhorsepublishing.com.

10 9 8 7 6 5 4 3 2 1

Library of Congress Cataloging-in-Publication Data is available on file.

Cover design by Jenny Zemanek
Cover illustration by iStock photo

Print ISBN: 978-1-5107-3881-2
Ebook ISBN: 978-1-5107-3882-9

Printed in China

To the strong women who had the courage to create something of their own by building a legacy through sisterhood;

to the mothers who are epic examples of strength and balance;

to the fathers who believe their daughters can be and do anything they dream;

to the brothers who respect and protect their sisters;

to the husbands who love, cherish, and celebrate their wives;

to the sisters created through grace and born in friendship;

to everyone who shares a passion for adventure;

these stories of girl power go out to you.

Table of Contents

My Dearest Sister

Some sisters are born into families, some are found in friendship, and others are forged by age-old traditions that emerged on college campuses centuries ago. We sorority girls don't buy our friends—we bond with them—because strong women aren't alone. We independent types weren't isolated yesterday, we still aren't today, and none of us will be tomorrow. Brainy chicks fighting gender roles in the early nineteenth century used to feel outnumbered on college campuses dominated by dudes. That's not the case anymore, and perhaps that's thanks to the sisterhood ancient coeds believed was necessary. Like men, women aren't only present in the classroom, at the office, and at home today. We are leaders, we have a voice, and, if we're lucky, we have some cute letters that will always remind us of our college glory days spent gallivanting around with the sisters we found in friendship.

LETTERS

Sister. You are not only a strong woman, you are the strongest tie to the best years of my life. Whether it's expressed via snail mail or in clever hashtags, our bond is not broken by an ever-growing and always evolving world; life changes only show just how much tradition means. We can better the lives of future girls like us by continuing to be ourselves and by helping one another stay true to those selves. We  can do that by remembering what girl power's all about. Whether our letters are proudly sported on T-shirts that are still in our everyday rotation or if they are tucked safely away in our adult attics long after we graduate, they mean something, and they always will. They are branded on our hearts like an adorable tattoo we'll never regret.

LEGACY

Thanks for giving me a chance to show you just how awesome and fabulous I can be, sister, and thanks for believing in me as a person. As gal pals, we don't see just how cool we are now; we can laugh at how nerdy we once were or imagine how great we'll one day be. We are the real deal. We'll inform one another (hopefully kindly), when a trendy haircut was a bad choice or when an eyeliner application was an epic fail. With cat eyes or as cat ladies, with or without makeup, while studying to become better or saddling up to prove it, when giggling and after panicking, whether our nails are done or when we're just done, *period*, with whatever drama is brewing, we've seen what makes each other break and what makes us shine.

YOU KNOW ME

You are my conscience, my partner in crime, my classroom companion, and the support system I know I need in the real world. Our friendship is bound to grow like the flower that reminds us of our sorority chapter, and that's the beauty of our relationship; it does not depart with the seasons, but it is reborn each time we embrace new chapters that have yet to be written. Our futures may not be certain, but we can take comfort in knowing our college stories are lasting. They will always remind us of the good times we shared and the laughter that lit up our nights, early mornings, and stressful schedules cluttered with classes.

WRITTEN FOR US

There is no need to stress about the term papers we don't have time to write. Our lives will write themselves. We can read and edit them at our leisure. It doesn't matter where we end up. I know how our friendship began. Thank you for being there for all of it. Thank you for helping me through the good times and the bad by picking me up when I was down, waking me up when I slept through my alarm, and keeping me up when you had gossip you knew I couldn't resist.

TRADITION

Our paths are linked by legacy and tradition. Becoming a grown-up is tough—being an adult is more like an acting gig we're trying to master with no formal training. Wherever we are in life, staying true to our friendship and the bonds we built in sisterhood may not always be as simple as opening the door to the sorority house for a chapter meeting, though it's safe to say we can't forget just how much walking through that door means in the grand scheme of our paths in life.

CHAPTERS

Our sorority chapter is just one story among many. The pages of sisterhood are composed of strong female characters, funny sidekicks, and inspiring heroines. We're the best of friends, but we each have our own life story. It's not written in our bylaws that I am your sidekick or you are mine. We are each other's supporting characters. Depending on the day, you might be in my story or I might be in yours. The important thing is that we both realize and respect that it's not always about us. In fact, as life goes on, it will be less about us and more about other stuff. Friendships evolve, and that's why we should identify this treasured time as a chapter to hold dear.

A LIFELONG PLEDGE OF SISTERHOOD

Girl power isn't an idea, it's a reality built on the experiences we have had and the trust we have established. Putting on a pretty face, paying dues, and participating in philanthropic pursuits is only part of the deal. In between these pages, lifelong friendships are born and continue to thrive. Thank you, my dearest sister, for reminding me that I am strong, inspiring me to be kind, leading me to pursue my dreams, helping me see how important it is to help others, encouraging me to grow in my own unique ways, and promising to be my friend in college and long after. I aspire to be the best sister I can be—wherever we end up—this is my heartfelt pledge of sisterhood.

My Dearest Sister

This is our sorority:

_____

_____

_____

_____

_____

These are our letters:

_____

_____

_____

_____

_____

We are known for:

_____

_____

_____

_____

_____

This is our sorority tagline:

_____

_____

_____

_____

_____

This is our open motto:

_____

_____

_____

_____

_____

I am thankful for:

_____

_____

_____

_____

_____

Chapter One

FOUNDED ON GIRL POWER

Sororities are not only a celebration of women, but also of individuals aspiring to shape meaningful lives and a better world. Does the sorority make the girl, or do the girls make the sorority? When it's a little bit of both, the result is not just one tough chick—it's a bunch of them. This herd isn't an aggressive stereotype of feminist freedom fighters who have a bone to pick with society. Rather, it's a fabulous collaboration of women seeking equality among men. We are well-rounded, unpredictable, independent, unique, and modestly awesome. We notice the irony in life, and we celebrate our place in it. We come in all shapes and sizes and have our own personal goals, but what makes sorority women special is that individuals can come together in support and creation of our common goals as women—one ambitious girl at a time.

PASTE IN A KEEPSAKE OF
YOU AND YOUR GIRLS

The Beginning of a Movement

In the 1946 Broadway musical *Annie Get Your Gun*, a female singer confidently belts the words, "Anything you can do, I can do better." A modern-day girl has to wonder if that's how the country's first sorority chicks felt. There is a distinct and obvious link between the origin of the first sororities (or, actually, female fraternities) and the evolution of a woman's fight to be taken seriously in the classroom, the workforce, and the world. Nearly seventy years before the Nineteenth Amendment earned women the right to vote, trailblazing intellectuals were planting the seeds for women's rights and independence by exuding girl power through prayer, song, and poetry as members of the first secret society for women. Now called Alpha Delta Pi, the Adelphean Society at Wesleyan Female College in Macon, Georgia laid the first foundation for sorority-style secret-society living way back in 1851.

SHH! IT'S A SECRET

Secret societies emerged on college campuses in the late eighteenth century because guys like Thomas Jefferson were seeking an outlet to expand their intellectual roots and social wings. They wanted to be able to discuss relevant issues of the day with their peers without stuffy professors censoring their debates. Created by dudes, for dudes, the Flat Hat Club (F.H.C.) Society was founded in 1750 at the College of William & Mary in Williamsburg, Virginia. It's likely that F.H.C. paid homage to a Latin phrase that means brotherhood, humanity, and knowledge. A triple threat, indeed!

SARCASTIC AND SMART SHOE-LOVERS

The birth of F.H.C. predates the Adelphean Society by ninety-nine years. It's not like women are impatient (or sarcastic). Imagine where women would be today if we hadn't been waiting around for one hundred years, clicking our heels together, daydreaming of when we'd have a chance to walk alongside men in theory and reality. It's not our fault we need more pairs of shoes to make strides toward our goals. Is that why men were so hesitant to accept a girl's place in higher education and the workforce? They knew we'd have another excuse to go shoe shopping?

SEEKING INDEPENDENCE

F.H.C.'s letters weren't Greek, but they stood for something, just like most Greek ones that came after. Could these brainy brother types like Jefferson have been foreshadowing a future of millennials only speaking in acronyms, long before social media was a thing and the instant gratification of a phone-in-hand was the norm? In Jefferson's day, college kids couldn't go around voicing all their opinions about everything. There wasn't a platform for all to banter, and not all banter was proper. What would Jefferson have thought about today's Internet communication tendencies? What would he have used as his social media profile picture? A melodramatic, black-and-white portrait of him staring longingly out a snowy window? He'd probably be thinking about how long it would take women to declare their independence, too.

ACADEMIC ACHIEVEMENT

Phi Beta Kappa was the first college society to generate its name from Greek letters. Like the Flat Hat Club, Phi Beta Kappa was created at the College of William & Mary. The first meeting was held in 1776 and the society's first president, John Heath, had a vision of building a legacy that was more serious-minded than the societies that came before. Phi Beta Kappa's commitment to scholarship is emblematic of what the society has evolved to become: one of the most prestigious honor societies in the country. Men and women selected as inductees to the Phi Beta Kappa Society are recognized as having attained impressive academic achievements in the liberal arts and sciences. Today there are more than 250 chapters of Phi Beta Kappa at colleges and universities across America. The first to induct women were at the University of Vermont in 1875, and at Connecticut's Wesleyan University in 1876.

THE START OF A BRIGHT FUTURE

While Alpha Delta Pi can claim credit as the first secret society, Phi Mu originated a year later in 1852 as the Philomathean Society at the same school. The term Philomathean is derived from the Greek *Philomath*, meaning "lover of learning." Social culture is a piece of sorority life, but a desire for education is at the heart of what sparked this entire sisterhood phenomenon. Pi Beta Phi was the first national fraternity for college chicks and it was founded in 1867. Kappa Alpha Theta was the first female Greek letter society founded in 1870 with Kappa Kappa Gamma following suit that same year.

A CHICK-ACHIEVEMENT

Kappa Alpha Thetas, also known as Thetas, were the first female inductees into Phi Beta Kappa. Bettie Locke Hamilton was one of Theta's founders. The concept for a Greek-letter fraternity was Bettie's, and she wasn't just a thinker, she was a doer and a leader. As an older woman, she reflected on the experience of founding a female fraternity at a time when women weren't supposed to be thinkers, doers, and leaders—especially on college campuses:

> You know the fraternity (Kappa Alpha Theta) was always second in my mind to coeducation. It was organized to help the girls win out in their fight to stay in college on a man's campus. We had to make a place for women in a man's world, and the fraternity was one means to that bigger end.

The words of Bettie Locke Hamilton continue to inspire women many years later and will always be a powerful citation in the story of how women found their strength in sorority.

A VOICE FOR FUTURE GIRLS

Thanks to feisty ladies of yesteryear, modern-day Annies got their glue guns. At a time when women were forging their places in higher education and their presence in the classroom was a controversial topic of discussion, forward-thinking chicks on college campuses knew they needed to team up to harness girl power. If they had to be silent in the classroom so as not to disturb the boys trying to learn, girls were going to seek out secret societies, just like the boys, so they too could have a voice. What began as a whisper of equality evolved to prove how much women can do when given the chance (and the right shoes). Incredible women were making strides back then and continue to do so today.

Founded on Girl Power

Our founders' names are:

_____

_____

_____

_____

_____

Founder's Day date is:

_____

_____

_____

_____

This is the time and place we were founded:

_____

_____

_____

_____

_____

Our school name is:

_____

_____

_____

_____

_____

Our school chapter name is:

_____

_____

_____

_____

_____

Our chapter house name is:

_____

_____

_____

_____

_____

Generations of Girl Power

Would the Nineteenth Amendment have ever been possible without Carrie Chapman Catt's commitment to suffrage and women's rights? Could her strength of character be traced back to her membership to the Pi Beta Phi chapter at Iowa State University? Catt was one of many women, some former sorority girls, fighting for suffrage. Perhaps the ones who went on to become famous politicians, actresses, astronauts, Supreme Court justices, fashion icons, and all-around good people can link their successes back to their sorority days.

FORWARD-THINKING FEMALES

Today there are more than four million sorority women in the world. That number exists because the strong few of the past had a great idea: to organize a gathering of women from different college campuses and unite in one common cause. Pretty impressive forward thinking considering the girls officially beat the guys to the punch by seven years. Whereas the National Panhellenic Conference for women's fraternities began in 1902, the National Interfraternity Conference for men's fraternities wasn't organized until 1909. Leave it to the ladies to show up late to the party and finally get it started when we arrive!

COMMON GROUND

Female college students of the late 1800s shared common ground at different locations and as members of different female fraternities. In 1891, Kappa Kappa Gamma invited all Greek-letter women's organizations in existence at the time to meet in Boston and collaborate on different sorority items and compare scars, so to speak. Two years later in 1893 there was a second meeting, except there is no record of it and only a few representatives showed up. Girls knew some kind of synergy needed to happen, but it wasn't until almost a decade later that Alpha Phi took charge of making it happen.

Sorority Girls Unite!

The National Panhellenic Conference took shape in the windy city in May 1902 after Alpha Phi welcomed eight other Greek-letter organizations to come and discuss relevant sorority-related issues like recruitment. Alpha Phi, Pi Beta Phi, Kappa Alpha Theta, Kappa Kappa Gamma, Delta Gamma, Gamma Phi Beta, and Delta Delta Delta were all in attendance. While Alpha Chi Omega and Chi Omega couldn't make the trip, they later jumped on board. This meeting has been credited with producing the first Interfraternity Association and first intergroup organization on college campuses. You go, girls!

BEING BRILLIANT IS A FULL-TIME JOB

Women can be the first to create a great idea of collaborating and building an alliance, but it's still going to take them half a century to decide on a name for it. It took boy fraternities more than one hundred years to realize it would be a good idea to build a conference between them, so who is going to criticize the trailblazing chicks who were a little wishy-washy about what to call it? Being brilliant is a full-time job, and women had a lot on their plates back then. No judgment here, just a whole lot of understanding. Being a woman is exhausting.

WHAT TO CALL THE STRONGEST WOMEN?

The National Panhellenic Conference (NPC) was first known as the Interfraternity Conference. It was renamed the Inter-Sorority Conference (ISC) in 1902, then changed to the National Panhellenic Conference in 1908, then changed *again* three years later to the National Panhellenic Congress in 1911. It stayed seriously committed to its new name for six years, until 1917 when the relationship became complicated again.

IT'S COMPLICATED, OKAY?

These girls were way ahead of social media relationship statuses, but with the odds they were up against, who could blame them? Sometimes we, as women, just need more time to analyze and think about what we really want. NPC's name went back to the National

Panhellenic Conference in 1917, then back again to the National Panhellenic Congress from 1921 until 1945, when it was decided that the National Panhellenic Conference made the most sense.

DECISIONS, DECISIONS

It's like searching for a prom dress in high school—going to thirty shops isn't going to make you change your mind about that first one you put on. Still, we need to know it's perfect! No matter what it was called over time, it's been the National Panhellenic Conference (NPC) since 1945 and this group of female leaders has always played a significant role in shaping the success of sorority women. NPC governs twenty-six international Greek-letter women's sororities and they are all amazing with their own unique traditions, histories, and values.

KEEPING A BALANCE

Secret societies may have been founded by men, but flexible, strong-willed women put their own spin on the same supportive concept. Providing equal opportunity for both is what keeps a balance in the world, our marriages, and on college campuses. Most men of the past could barely fathom girls attending college, let alone a woman becoming a professor or a dean. It's a far cry from where we are today in a time when strength takes many forms. Modern-day women are running for president. Men *and* women are voting for them. This is a world that sorority pioneers dreamed of before women had a seat at any table that wasn't holding up a hot dinner.

FIGHTING FOR COMFORT

The beauty of being a college coed today is that the fears once keeping women out of higher education classrooms are no longer coming to fruition; they are simply manifested into proof of our strength, potential, and ability to multitask. In spite of everything women have to juggle, we can study stuff and problem solve, too. We *can* make a difference! Is it really such a stretch to think that women can change the world for the better? Men of today have certainly relaxed into that truth, and some dudes even believed in this possibility long before society accepted it as such.

EVER HEARD OF ESTROGEN?

Getting a seat in the lecture hall wasn't always easy for women battling the odds. Most guys back then were convinced chicks would have nervous breakdowns if they had to compete in a man's world. Maybe the men were just weary of competing with their "crazy" female counterparts or couldn't imagine dealing with all the girls in their classes syncing up their menstrual cycles at the same time. Who could blame men for being afraid of that? Women are powerful when our goals are in sync.

MENTAL MENSTRUATION

Can women really menstruate and think? By golly, it sucks, but it's possible. Female students today certainly have the right to pull the covers over their eyes when Cousin Flo pays a monthly visit, making class attendance seem impossible with a cramping tummy and a crummy hormonal imbalance that's fogging the brain and its thoughtful prowess. Luckily, playing hooky once in a while is a modern-day luxury bequeathed to us from determined women of the past.

WEARING THE PANTS

Newsflash to the past: women and men can both wear the pants in the family. Trying to work a job during the day and put food on the table at night after moseying around in a ball gown for twelve hours sounds glamorous, but totally impractical. It's just like all the lies modern-day college girls tell themselves about thongs being their most comfortable underwear; every thirty-year-old woman knows that's a bunch of garbage. If women still wore the layered garb of the 1800s, there's no way New York City could fit a bunch of them into a subway car—a tough truth for a world now reliant on working women—though it might be a funny viral video to record and share with the masses.

PROUD TO WEAR THE PANTS

Life says we have to pay the bills somehow, and ball gowns are kind of expensive, so that's a moot point for an everyday wardrobe. *Sigh.* Alas, we shouldn't hold anything against men of the early nineteenth century. How could they have ever predicted how cute we'd look in skinny jeans and yoga pants? Sure, maybe we choose comfort when we roll out to class or to the department store to pick up a few things, but we still get the job done—and look (and feel) damn good while doing it!

SING IT, GIRL!

Back when Sigma Kappa was founded at Colby College in Waterville, Maine, women didn't exactly feel welcomed by all their male classmates. It was 1874, Colby College was the first college in New England to admit women on an equal basis with male students, and disgruntled dudes spared no feelings when standing up for the old ways. This was a practice not limited to Colby. When Indiana Asbury College (now DePauw University) opened its Greencastle, Indiana campus to women in 1867, people feared the acceptance of females would diminish the college's reputation. Many coed campuses of the era were cold with an unwillingness to change, but women didn't bring down the house—we helped build it. A modern-day diva should write a song about that!

TO LOOK GOOD, BUT NOT TOO GOOD

Nobody should apologize for looking good while solving a math problem, and nobody should be expected to look good after studying all night. Wouldn't ball gowns, parasols, and thousands of layers be a little over-the-top for deep-thinking debates, even way back when? What a distraction! (The attire, not the women.) How would women fit into lecture hall chairs with all that heavy fabric? How would we pee without help from another girl on campus? Is that why women of the past were forced to sit behind sheets or walls so that men could focus on learning, and is that why girls today are so keen on going to the bathroom in groups? One thing is certain: early coed classrooms weren't happy about women speaking and participating in discussions. No wonder these ladies sought out secret societies so that they could catch up on how dumb that was.

FEISTY FEMALES

Feeling and thinking at the same time is what makes women so darn cunning. It's a fortifying structure that transforms women into empathetic yet confident wives, mothers, sisters, and daughters. Today, we are balancing the traditional roles with more modern ones, and hopefully our husbands are helping us keep our sanity, or we single gals have yoga or some other outlet to organize our many thoughts. Otherwise, we might prove the ancient guy's manifesto of us being crazy right, and nobody wants to prove crazy right.

PROGRESSIVE THOUGHTS

Women of the past had a lot to deal with, and while we've obviously progressed, there's still much to manage today, especially in a culture that expects women to do it all. Any hormonal woman that's nearly lost it after unloading a full shopping cart into the car (that is, if she can even find her car in the parking lot) and realizing she forgot the one thing she needed can sympathize. Handling the pressure in a mature and educated way helps us live out the dreams of the first sorority girls and keeps us from becoming that viral video of the crazy lady that lost her mind in the supermarket check-out line.

BUILDING THE FOUNDATION FOR MODERN MOMS

Today, women know how to juggle, and we even make time to share our successes and failures on social media while we're vacuuming or making Mickey Mouse pancakes. Back in the day, women were controlled by societal norms and only went to school to become better wives and mothers. It was all about finishing schools and focusing on the family. Women craved an intellectual challenge, just as women of today crave a break from intellectual challenges (Ahem: reality TV). Anyway, presumably there weren't any Rubik's cubes or magazine quizzes at the time of sorority girl birth, and these ladies wanted more mindful material, anyway. That was the whole point, wasn't it? They took fate into their own hands and laid the groundwork so that we could have a reason to need a mental break from all the thinking we do now.

Crafting Tip

SORORITY PADDLES

Paddles are a big part of sorority crafting and a prime symbol of sisterhood. It's hard not to notice that they are shaped a lot like a bottle of wine, or maybe bottles of wine are shaped like paddles. Either way, why not repurpose, repaint, and un-bedazzle your paddle? Buying a wine plaque can be expensive, and a paddle really is the spitting image of the outline. You can trade in the bright colors from your sorority days for more neutral hues to suit your adult style and wine tastes. Speaking of wine, save the corks! You could make a monogram letter of your name or your sorority, or you could create an epic corkboard. If you aren't about those grapes, think about recrafting your paddle as a hat rack, coat rack, or jewelry holder. If you're sentimental about your paddle and clueless on crafts, take a picture of your paddle and keep that as your keepsake. If all this sounds awful, throw your paddle into the woods, off a cliff, or deep into the restricted section of your attic, and call it a day. It's made of wood, so it will blend. Just make sure you don't accidentally hit anyone in the head with it.

SORORITY PADDLES (THEN)

SORORITY PADDLES (NOW)

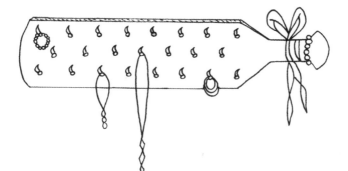

A NEW AGE OF WOMEN

In a 1907 edition of Alpha Delta Pi's quarterly magazine, the *Adelphean*, Mrs. Edgar Ross (Alpha Chapter) wrote, "Be ready to show the world that Adelphean—in both English and Greek—spells lady, and woman in the strongest sense." Today, there are all kinds of strong women carving out their own definitions of strength. Some of us are naturally great in the kitchen, while others wouldn't mind picking up some life hacks about convincing others we know how to cook. We might be powerful, but are we superhuman? Sometimes saying *Bam!* as the microwave door shuts just doesn't feel like enough. With all that pressure riding on the first college coeds and sorority girls, it's no wonder working women and stay-at-home mothers are so hard on themselves today. We just have different pressures now, and we're all unique in our expectations of what makes us viable women. Thankfully, sorority women have networks. We can learn from our past and be inspired by it! Sororities aren't just about women supporting women, they are about women working with both men and women to make the world a better place. That's why sororities are fabulous beyond the confines of their campuses.

PASTE IN A KEEPSAKE OF
YOU AND YOUR GUYS

A New Age of Women

This is our mascot:

_____

_____

_____

_____

_____

This is our jewel:

_____

_____

_____

_____

_____

This is our badge:

_____

_____

_____

_____

_____

These are our colors:

_____

_____

_____

_____

_____

Our colors symbolize:

_____

_____

_____

_____

_____

A symbol of our sorority is:

_____

_____

_____

_____

_____

More than a Sisterhood: A Family

In 1851, a young, wide-eyed Eugenia Tucker was sixteen years old and quite the go-getter. Along with five other young women at Wesleyan University in Macon, Georgia, Tucker helped found the first secret society for women on a college campus, the Adelphean Society, now known as Alpha Delta Pi. Talk about chicks too legit to quit! After graduating as the valedictorian of her class, Tucker lived a long life and was widowed twice. Though she had no biological children of her own, Eugenia Tucker Fitzgerald was considered a mother to many. In the March 1907 edition of the *Adelphean*, "Mother Fitzgerald" wrote a message to her girls, warning them not to ignore their sacred duties as mothers, daughters, wives, and sisters. Women of all times have felt a duty to play many roles and be everything to everyone. Sorority sisters can help keep a girl in check and remind her it's okay to be human.

THE WEIGHT OF THE WORLD

Women waited long enough not to have the weight of the world fall on their shoulders. While it's empowering to seek independence in professional accomplishments, we can easily get lost in the crusade of going after our dreams. Being a humble yet driven woman is a dynamic, twofold entity many sororities preach as a well-rounded truth. Living up to the expectations of others sometimes feels impossible, but sororities can teach a girl how to create her own expectations. There is no right answer. Not all women need or want to be mothers. Not all women are compelled to find self-completion in career milestones. A woman is not an actress being cast into a role—she is the director of her own life.

MOTHER MAY I?

Many mothers of the 1800s saw their daughters' futures plain and simple: marriage was a happy ending. "I do" meant I don't need personal or professional development outside the house. Forward-thinking moms like Margaret E. Armitage Dodge had another notion: if men were to benefit from having a college education, her bright daughter should do the same, and with her mother's support, she surely did. Helen Mary Dodge became one of four founding sisters of Gamma Phi Beta at Syracuse University in 1874. It just so happens that her sorority was the first to be called such!

A FEMININE NAME FOR A FEMALE FRATERNITY

Until 1882, men's and women's organizations were both referred to as fraternities, but fraternity didn't sound feminine enough for some of the girls involved. Unimpressed with the frat girl connotation, they would often refer to their organizations as societies instead. Being equal, but different, is an important piece of celebrating the bonds of brotherhood and sisterhood. Gamma Phi Beta was the first sorority to be called a sorority, meaning sisterhood. The person who coined the term was a Professor Smalley—and he was a dude! Not all men back then had notions about keeping women in the kitchen and out of college. How refreshing it must have been for the girls to know a guy was in their corner, too. Professor Frank Smalley congratulated his students when they announced the installation of Gamma Phi Beta at Syracuse, calling their group a sorority for the first time. The feminine-sounding term stuck, and the rest is history.

A SORORITY GIRL BECOMES A MOTHERLY FIGURE

Tri Delta, or Delta Delta Delta, was founded at Boston University in 1888 and was the first female fraternity to write all ritual without the help of any men. Woot! Sarah Ida Shaw was one of four founders and would go on to become a name to remember in sorority history, authoring *The Sorority Handbook* and guiding future generations of college chicks down the right path.

After marriage, she would have become Sarah Ida Shaw Martin, except she dropped Sarah which saved her from having to sign four names or introduce herself four times, which sounds exhausting. Some sorority founders had names long enough to make a modern girl thank her lucky stars for the acceptance of acronyms and one-word monikers.

A SORORITY MOM

Martin was basically a sorority (soccer) mom. She may not have driven a big van but she was all about giving others a lift. She also helped the struggling Alpha Sigma Alpha (founded in 1901 at the State Female Normal School in Farmville, Virginia) reorganize and refocus by expanding to teacher's colleges and schools of education within universities. Her work with Alpha Sigma Alpha was so dedicated that she eventually became an honorary member and national president. She is also credited with helping Zeta Tau Alpha Fraternity (founded in 1898 also at the State Female Normal School) expand to northern chapters and become a member of NPC.

A PLACE FOR OTHER MOTHERS

In 1914, mothers of the Delta Lambda chapter of Tri Delta at Butler College in Indianapolis met up and made their own sorority! Ida Shaw Martin served as a counselor (did that make her a grandmother?) and guide of Psi Psi Psi, the only Greek letter mother's sorority and the only international sorority of mothers of fraternity women. Meanwhile, Alpha Phi has a special program that allows the mothers of members to be initiated into Alpha Phi membership with their daughters. As long as the moms aren't affiliated with another NPC group, they are welcome to join.

MOTHERS AND FATHERS

The first mother's club of Phi Mu Fraternity was formed by the Eta Alpha Chapter at the University of California/Berkley in 1921. Because many fathers became very interested in their daughters' collegiate pursuits, mothers' clubs were changed to parents' associations in 1978. Such a well-intended symbol of the changing roles of men and women makes a girl want to give her dad a big hug!

More Than a Sisterhood: A Family

Our sorority is the best because:

_____

_____

_____

_____

Our sorority rival(s) is/are:

_____

_____

_____

_____

Our favorite fraternity to mix with is:

_____

_____

_____

_____

Our badge represents:

_____

_____

_____

_____

_____

Our core values are:

_____

_____

_____

_____

_____

Our ritual is:

_____

_____

_____

_____

_____

Guy Pals for Goal-Driven Gals

Syracuse's Professor Smalley wasn't the only guy big enough to see what women could do if given the chance. In fact, the early days of many female fraternities (and sororities) are tied to the helping hand of a man who could see past the social barriers of the day. Many male professors, students, fathers, and brothers played key supporting roles in helping female fraternities and sororities get off the ground.

FAITHFUL FATHERS

The relationship between a father and a daughter is unique, precious, and different for everyone. With the changing structure of social norms and expectations for young women during the founding days of female fraternities, fathers were either their daughters' biggest fans or strongest critics. Either way, strong women were becoming stronger as daddy's little girl grew into a new kind of woman.

TRAILBLAZING DAD

One of Alpha Delta Pi's founders, Ella Pierce Turner, was the daughter of Dr. George Foster Pierce. This guy served as the first president of Wesleyan Female College in Macon, Georgia— the first college in the world chartered to grant degrees to women.

HERO NEIGHBOR DAD

In 1867, Pi Beta Phi Fraternity was founded as I.C. Sorosis at Monmouth College in Monmouth, Illinois, in the home of Major Jacob H. Holt because two of the organization's founders were renting rooms there. As a result, the Holt House has held a lot of history and meaning in the hearts of Pi Beta Phi girls for years to come. As years passed, the Holt family's last surviving ancestor,

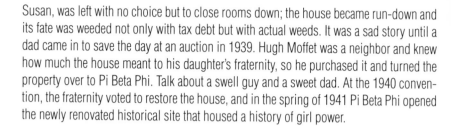

Susan, was left with no choice but to close rooms down; the house became run-down and its fate was weeded not only with tax debt but with actual weeds. It was a sad story until a dad came in to save the day at an auction in 1939. Hugh Moffet was a neighbor and knew how much the house meant to his daughter's fraternity, so he purchased it and turned the property over to Pi Beta Phi. Talk about a swell guy and a sweet dad. At the 1940 convention, the fraternity voted to restore the house, and in the spring of 1941 Pi Beta Phi opened the newly renovated historical site that housed a history of girl power.

A DAD AND SOME BROTHERS

In 1870, Kappa Alpha Theta was founded at Indiana University, now DePauw University, in Indianapolis, Indiana. Bettie Locke Hamilton (one of the four female founders) helped lead the way. Her father was a professor and member of Beta Theta Pi, while her brother belonged to Phi Gamma Delta (FIJI). Because she had quite a few friends in FIJI, the brothers asked Bettie to wear their badge, but inspired by her father and brother, she craved a club of her own. Bettie asked if wearing FIJI's badge would make her a member of the fraternity, and after some serious deliberation, the boys reluctantly and very politely said no—it was for dudes only. The badge would have been a symbol of friendship, like a varsity jacket today, perhaps, but not a real membership card (sort of like a free trial to an Internet program that doesn't quite grant you anything cool). Bettie and the boys had an amicable exchange. She politely declined, and they gave her a fruit basket, which is a timeless symbol of sorry, let's still be friends. Anyway, with the help of her father, Bettie started Kappa Alpha Theta, and it's been awesome ever since.

A FATHER OF FAITH

In 1909, Father Edward D. Kelly had a vision of a positive outlet for Catholic women at the University of Michigan. He created Omega Upsilon for Catholic women, but by the spring of 1912, membership was kind of failing. That's when he reached out to Michigan alum Amelia McSweeney. With the help of seven other alumni and the addition of two interested undergraduates, McSweeney reorganized things and Theta Pi Alpha Fraternity was founded in 1912.

SWEET DUDES OF SYRACUSE

Gamma Phi Beta's colors, mode and brown, are an ode to a kind man. Mode is basically a lighter version of a particular color but sounds way more impressive than simply saying light brown. Light brown is boring. Girls aren't boring. We're fascinating. Anyway, Dr. John J. Brown was another Syracuse professor who offered support to the go-getting girls of the day by extending the use of his parlor room as a meeting place. Gamma Phi Beta girls first declined the offer because there were members of another sorority (Alpha Phi) living in Brown's house. They didn't want their secrets revealed. The Gamma Phi girls later took Brown up on his generosity and felt so indebted to him that they decided on a brown palette. The subdued shades were vibrant in spirit and meaning, and that was plenty.

A SAFE HAVEN FOR WOMEN IN HIGHER EDUCATION

One of Gamma Phi Beta's founders, Frances Elizabeth Haven, was the daughter of Erastus O. Haven, the Chancellor of Syracuse and a man who encouraged his daughter to go after her goals. Before serving in his role at Syracuse, Haven was the president of Northwestern University. He would only accept that job on the account that women would be allowed to attend school there. Talk about a dad looking out for the best interests of his daughter!

EVEN STRONG WOMEN NEED ROOFS OVER THEIR HEADS

Founded in 1872, Alpha Phi girls found support in fatherly figures and brotherhood, too. Dr. Wellesley Coddington was a Greek and philosophy professor who offered guidance and friendship to Alpha Phi girls because he was all about chicks learning stuff and leading others. He even encouraged the girls of Alpha Phi to rent and build a chapter house and introduced them to one of their most famous initiates: women's suffrage champ Frances E. Willard. In 1886, Alpha Phi became the first women's fraternity in America to build and occupy a chapter house. Humble and wise is the man who can unite strong women together!

BEST MAN IN A SUPPORTING ROLE

They say that behind every powerful man is a smart woman. Perhaps that saying goes both ways. By 1901, all founding organizations of NPC had a chapter at Syracuse University. This Coddington character had a hand in the founding of Alpha Gamma Delta at Syracuse in 1904. Alpha Gamma Delta was founded on May 30th that year in Coddington's home.

Beyond Sisters

Phi Sigma Sigma was founded in 1913 at Hunter College in New York City. The founders of the first nonsectarian society believed that women of different faiths could band together and support one another's goals. The brotherhood of man was one of their twin ideals, striking a heartfelt chord in the belief that sometimes sisterhood is a bond that goes beyond sisters. In fact, some men have been so loyal that powerful yet humble women cannot help but give credit where credit is due. Some brothers are more than friends—they are family.

AN HONORARY DUDE

Delta Gamma was founded in 1873 at the Lewis School for Girls in Oxford, Mississippi. In the early days of DG, the organization had trouble expanding beyond the South. That is, until George Banta brought Delta Gamma home to Indiana. A guest speaker at many Delta Gamma conventions and a member of Phi Delta Theta fraternity, Banta assisted with the rewriting of DG's ritual and helped bring Delta Gamma to Franklin College, his alma mater. Banta's fiancée, Lillie Vawter, was the first DG initiate to the Phi chapter, named in honor of Banta's membership in Phi Delta Theta. Banta married his college sweetheart in 1882 and became an honorary member of Delta Gamma. To think, the combo hashtags these two lovebirds could have concocted had social media been a thing at the time of their wedding!

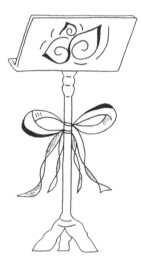

A SHARED HISTORY

In 1893, Alpha Xi Delta was founded at Lombard College in Galesburg, Illinois. Alpha Xi Delta has long held a special bond with what could be considered its brother fraternity, Sigma Nu. It turns out that the early days of Lombard College had a lot of gallivanting between Phi Delta Theta, a frat for dudes, and Pi Beta Phi, a frat for chicks. Sigma Nu was happy to welcome a new sorority on campus, so when Alpha Xi Delta showed up, the pair quickly forged a bond. A Sigma Nu alum named James J. Welsh helped the girls draft a constitution, and Albert H. (Bert) Wilson helped Alpha Xi Delta expand to other campuses. Wilson continued on to assist Mary Emily Kay, a student at Mount Union College in Ohio, draft a successful petition. She was initiated in 1902 and became Alpha Xi Delta's fourth national president. "Inspiring Women to Realize their Potential" became Alpha Xi Delta's powerfully fitting vision.

CARRYING THE TORCH

Sigma Delta Tau was founded at Cornell University in 1917, and since then there's been just one man lucky enough to don the SDT Torch Pin. An idealistic and poetically inclined Nathan Caleb House was the perfect person to help members of SDT with the writing of their ritual. Though he briefly went MIA after graduation, a sister found him in the NYC phone book, and his SDT story continued. He became known as Brother Nat after maintaining connections with many alumnae and collegiate chapters.

A TRIPLE THREAT'S HELPING HAND

Sigma Sigma Sigma, or Tri-Sigma, was founded in 1898 at the State Female Normal College in Farmville, Virginia. J. Miller Leake, a member of Kappa Sigma at Randolph-Macon Men's College, wrote the sorority's initiation ritual, helped revise the constitution, and assisted in writing lyrics to a couple of songs. Leake was the only guy permitted to wear the indented triangle badge of Tri Sig.

SORORITY CHEERLEADERS

Alpha Chi Omega was founded in 1885 at DePauw University in Indianapolis, Indiana. It was the first Greek letter society for women enrolled in a music school, and the founders were encouraged by the dean of DePauw's School of Music to form a women's society within the school. This dude dean, also known as Professor James Hamilton Howe, even wore the sorority colors on the lapel of his coat to honor the scarlet red and olive green shades of Alpha Chi Omega. It seems like that would be the sophisticated equivalent of him wearing a team bride sash or carrying a girl power flag around campus today.

A DENTAL RAPPER

In 1895, Chi Omega was founded at the University of Arkansas. Dr. Charles Richardson was a local dentist who earned the legendary title Sis Doc to generations of members of the founding chapter. Sis Doc sounds like a 1990s rapper name, but his time came a century before that when he drafted the constitution and bylaws of Chi Omega and crafted the group's first badge out of dental gold! He is credited as one of the founders of the organization—and you know it's legit because the dude has it written on his gravestone in Fayetteville, Arkansas.

A DOCTOR OF A DIFFERENT KIND

The only guy allowed to wear the Delta Zeta badge was named Dr. Guy Potter Benton. Benton was the 13th president of Miami University in Ohio, a grand patron of DZ, and a key player in preparing the sorority's ritual.

THE GRACE OF FAMILY

While sorority women certainly had to muster up their own courage, gumption, and ambition from within to even consider attending college in the first place, it's comforting to think about all the protagonists and supporting characters who played a significant role in their story of triumph. As young women petitioned to find a place for themselves as new kinds of women, it's important to honor the people who fought on their behalf. Going against the norm is never an easy decision

and is one that takes guts. Where would sorority women be today without the support of friends and family? While the majority of ancient folks might not have welcomed women to campus, there were countless helping hands who believed women could make a difference in the future and deserved to be there at the time. There were fathers, brothers, and relationships forged in friendship with both peers and mentors that gave these women the confidence to keep pursuing their vision of an equal future. There were mothers and older women that passed a torch of female empowerment, hoping their daughters could have access to more than they did by encouraging them to pursue their passions. Could women have done it without the help of others? One can only imagine it would have taken women much longer to get to where we are now— and for all the help, we are thankful.

Crafting Tip

LETTERS

Sorority girls have a knack for wearing thousands of T-shirts bearing letters, letters, and more letters! Letters in every color and pattern imaginable. The "What was I thinking?" letters and the "Classic bid day" letters are part of the same collection of college garb. Girls take their letters seriously. Representing your sorority with your letters was always a proud pick for an outfit in your college days, but should these once-cherished pieces of cotton end up in a box in your basement for the rest of post-college eternity? They very well could, but you could also transform them into a blanket, pillow, or tote bag—that is, if sewing is a feminine forte that doesn't haunt your dreams. If all this sounds like a brutal, tiny needle attack on your craft-lacking fingers, think about buying a shadow box frame and folding up your favorite T-shirt that has been deemed the chosen one. Center the letters in the frame, and you've got a meaningful keepsake for your home or office!

LETTERS (THEN)

LETTERS (NOW)

Chapter Three

SHARING A MEANINGFUL LIFE

There's an old joke about sorority girls having to pay for their friends. Every one of us has heard the intended insult from someone who scoffs at the concept of going Greek and assumes the higher road is one not taken down Frat Row. Hey—many sorority girls started out as those nonbelievers, but paying for your friends doesn't quite mean what people think. Life can be hard. There are some sororities that have programs in place to support girls who could use more than a shoulder to cry on when money gets tight. When a girl encounters the unthinkable, her sorority can be there to take the financial pressure off. Kappa Alpha Theta's Friendship Fund provides assistance to sisters feeling the weight of severe financial burdens caused by unexpected illnesses, natural disasters, or other unexpected tragedies. They aren't alone, and while most stubborn women wouldn't even think of asking for help, they've already got it. Even after college, as alumnae, sorority women have a support system in the true friends who will always acknowledge the lifelong dues they hold dear: the spirit of their sisterhood. Giving and helping others is ingrained in sorority girls. Each sorority has carved its own positive mark on humanity, and every organization has a history of women who have used that mark as a starting point to branch out and continue to make the world a better place. By being positive leaders, influencers, friends, daughters, wives, and, of course, sisters, sorority girls are paying their dues long after they graduate.

PASTE IN A KEEPSAKE
OF YOUR MOST MEANINGFUL
SORORITY MOMENT

Sharing a Meaningful Life

This is our philanthropy:

_____

_____

_____

_____

We are passionate about:

_____

_____

_____

_____

We are known for:

_____

_____

_____

_____

We fund-raise by:

_____

_____

_____

_____

_____

I can't believe we:

_____

_____

_____

_____

I am most proud of:

_____

_____

_____

_____

A Promise to Help

Does popular culture think the biggest crisis a letter-wearing college girl has to deal with is a broken nail or choosing an outfit for a hot date? Deciding which pair of shoes best matches a dress doesn't come close to the most difficult decision a girl has to make—we all know that. In fact, perhaps that's why some of us lose our minds over such a miniscule task, creating chaos out of our closets and making it look like our wardrobe threw up all over our bedroom floor. If our brains are beat down daily with bigger problems and decisions, it's no wonder we grow weary over the silly and small decisions. Some of us might be unable to sweat the small stuff, but at least most of us know when to "man" up.

MANNING UP

The concept of manning up is perhaps equally detrimental to both men and women. First, it suggests that men always need to be "men," as if they don't have a soul or a sentimental bone in their masculine bodies, which they obviously do, and as if admitting they do is some kind of dirty confession. Second, it suggests that being tough is primarily a man's job, when everyone knows that women, especially mothers, are fearless when it comes to protecting something or someone we care about. So men aren't allowed to show their emotions and women aren't allowed to conceal theirs? That's just silly. Anyone who has encountered a man knows that he can't always just have something in his eye. Anyone who's ever watched a show about nature knows that furry mom creatures of different breeds don't mess around when keeping their babies safe. Both men and women can be sentimental *and* tough. There is something powerful about a call to duty, especially when good-hearted people come together to fight for one common cause.

THE MORE IMPORTANT THINGS

The response of sorority women through trying times of natural disasters and two world wars supports a new phrase: to woman up. Let that mean something strong. The women who were making impactful strides toward a changing role for future gals stepped up when the time came to prove they weren't kidding around. They wanted to make a difference in the world. That's the basis on which sororities were founded, and that's what sorority women were going to do.

SUITING UP

Strong women have always been fighters and supporters during times of distress. During the Civil War, thousands of chicks on both sides of the line decided their dainty domestic duties didn't mean squat if all the men were dying on the battlefield. It was time to do something, so they joined volunteer brigades and worked as nurses. Others cooked and cleaned for soldiers. Then there were the hundreds of leading ladies that disguised themselves as men so they could fight alongside them on the front lines. With so many men having gone to battle, women at home rose to the challenge as schoolteachers. What was thought to be a temporary role evolved into a more permanent one, proving the need for women to attend college and join the ranks of men in higher education. The end of the Civil War coincides with the beginnings of some of the nation's oldest sororities, spotlighting the fact that women were redefining their place as versatile tough chicks with many cards to play at the table.

THE GREAT WAR

The First World War was a turning point for women from all sections of society in the United States, a time to show their patriotism by serving their country in a variety of ways. Roles varied; higher class women could be found devoting time to volunteer organizations while middle and lower class ladies worked tangible jobs at home and abroad. Isn't social classification, as a term, annoying? A girl's class should be determined by her poise and character, not her pocketbook. Anyway, some women became nurses and others filled in the gaps men left behind on the home front. Most women making a difference in the war effort wore uniforms as a symbol of their patriotism, and women of all classes became vested in doing something positive to help their country no matter their classification—how classy is that?

SORORITY CHICKS UNITE

Among the ranks of women supporting the war effort were sorority girls. Throughout their history, many sororities have shown a devoted interest in caring for underprivileged children in some way or another. Efforts by Greek organizations during the Great War are a prime example, as many chapters adopted war orphans or supported the needs of Belgian and French children overseas by raising money and sending donations. Alpha Chi Omega, Alpha Delta Pi, Alpha Gamma Delta, Alpha Omicron Pi, Delta Gamma, Delta Zeta, Gamma Phi Beta, Kappa Alpha Theta, Sigma Kappa, and Zeta Tau Alpha were among the many sororities playing a patriotic part in this regard. They weren't the only ones making a difference, and adopting war orphans was only one aspect of what they did to help. More than thirty members of Gamma Phi Beta journeyed to Europe to work for the Red Cross or the war department. Other organizations, like Pi Beta Phi, helped female foreigners studying in America cover costs for books, clothes, and travel. Notable Alpha Delta Pi alums Jeanette Barrows and Gladys Gilpatrick paid the ultimate sacrifice during the First World War. Barrows was a reconstruction aide who died while tending to the wounded, and Gilpatrick was an army nurse who perished while on active duty. Meanwhile, Kappa Alpha Theta alum Daisy Florence Simms was the first director of the Industrial Department of the National Board of the Young Women's Christian Association (YWCA), which mobilized businesswomen to train young women for positions left open in the business world after World War I. These stories are just tidbits of the vast amount of support sorority women provided during a war-torn time in America.

WORLD WAR II

Unfortunately, the "war to end all wars" wasn't the last war America would see. When the 1941 attack on Pearl Harbor led the United States into World War II, sorority women rose to the challenge in a number of ways. They set up women's service centers, volunteered at hospitals, assisted with bandage rolling and knitting for the Red Cross, participated in war bond drives, and held fund-raisers to aid wounded soldiers. Alpha Epsilon Phi presented an ambulance to the US Army and received a citation of patriotism from the US Treasury Department. Alpha Delta Pi alumna Mildred Tuttle Axton was the first woman in the civilian pilot training program in 1940 and served as a WASP World War II test pilot. She was one cool chick, but she wasn't alone in serving as a shining representation of the drive behind sorority women. Distinguished war correspondent Marguerite Higgins was a member of Gamma Phi Beta and later became the first woman to win a Pulitzer Prize for her brilliant international reporting during the Korean War in 1951 (she shared the award with five other dudes, all of whom had to be completely shocked and impressed by her feats). During World War II, she witnessed the release of prisoners from the Dachau concentration camp and covered the Nuremberg war trials. When one guy tried to tell her that she couldn't be in Korea covering man stuff, she appealed to his superior officer, who just happened to be General Douglas McArthur, who then sent a telegram to her place of employment, the *Herald Tribune*. McArthur praised Higgins for being awesome and said she belonged in the thick of things. Talk about guts. The next time any of us feels like she has it rough at her job, we should remember Higgins and be inspired by her fearless gumption.

DEVELOPING FEARLESS WOMEN

With the general mantra of sororities being about girl power, it's kind of a given that they kick butt at helping others. The philanthropic work of sororities is sincerely a push-and-pull effort that overcomes challenges and comforts those being challenged. The smiles of sorority sisters make the struggle others are dealing with feel a little less impossible and a little more supported. Sororities are emotionally, financially, and socially tied to their philanthropies and have raised millions of dollars and volunteer hours in order to make a difference.

A STUBBORN RIGHT

Women don't need to be tough all the time, but we'll become superhuman versions of ourselves when duty calls. Not all men or women loved the idea of women forging a new path alongside men, but that didn't stop determined chicks from making a difference, and it didn't stop supportive men from helping them out. Humans are complex. Perhaps our qualities are developed in part by those who influence our growth as individuals, and a strong girl will unknowingly acquire the best qualities from everyone around her in a subconscious mission to better herself. Sorority women can find inspiration in their fellow sisters and the trailblazing ones of the past who laid the foundation for a sisterhood rooted in service.

This is Our Creed/ Symphony/Purpose

A sorority creed, symphony, or purpose is not just a bunch of words. This vocabulary was specifically chosen—it means something special. These lines are written to recall the past and envision the future, to be read and spoken now as a motto for living in this moment. Like a song that empowers the heart to dance, a poem that moves the soul, a conviction that inspires the mind to think deeply, each sorority's mission is expressed uniquely, passionately, and purposefully. Write out your chapter creed, symphony, or purpose here!

Ladies Breaking Ground

Delta Gamma's founders began their sorority with a mission spelled by its own letters: DG. These girls wanted to "do good." The earliest sororities were founded on the opportunity to play a role in helping others, the chance to make a difference, and the potential to grow. These ideals were fuel for the sorority's social existence. It wasn't just about the support of friendship; it was about sealing friendship through a shared ministry of work and making a difference. Greek organizations

served as the catalyst, the reason, and the binding force to inspire women to be their best selves. They joined hands and reached out to help others as a unified front.

UNION HAND IN HAND

Union Hand in Hand is the public motto of Alpha Phi International Fraternity. Clara Sittser Williams was one of Alpha Phi's ten founders at Syracuse University. The daughter of a farmer, William spoke down-to-earth words that still ring true today. "We were to be ever loyal to one another, in joys or sorrows, success or failure . . . and ever extend a helping hand to our sisters who needed our aid . . . truly we planned to be a Union hand in hand." Back in 1902, it was Alpha Phi's invitation that brought Pi Beta Phi, Kappa Alpha Theta, Kappa Kappa Gamma, Delta Gamma, Gamma Phi Beta, and Delta Delta Delta together in Chicago. That meeting set the stage for more than a century of mutual understandings and began a powerful movement of women supporting women in their plight to earn a voice and a place in society. Though Alpha Chi Omega and Chi Omega couldn't make it to the original meeting, they soon became part of what the group evolved into: The National Panhellenic Conference. Creating an even playing ground for individuals to debate, discuss, and develop ideas means so much today, but it meant even more during the days of founding sorority women. Imagine the guts it took sorority chicks back then to proudly preach their intellect! How inspiring to know that they found one another and worked together to prove they were smarter than they seemed to society at the time.

A HUMBLE GROWTH

Women don't necessarily need to be in total agreement with one another in order to be supportive acquaintances. They don't have to wear the same clothes, bear the same crest, or carry the same badge to represent a common idea. The bonds between the sisters of other fraternities might not be the same as the ones developed within the sacred walls of a mutual fraternity, but they are still special and everlasting in their own way. While each of the NPC founding groups and current members has their own traditions, histories, symbols, and unique stories that set them apart, it is these very nuances, enigmas, and sacred tales that also unite them as kindred spirits. It's enlightening to be competitive

on college campuses; competition is fuel to become a better organization, just as friendly competition between sisters and friends can serve as inspiration to become better people. As Annette Holt Hitchcock (Pi, North Dakota) wrote in Alpha Phi's creed, penned in 1912:

I believe in my Fraternity
I believe in the friendships formed
in the springtime of my youth.
I believe in its high ideals
which lift me up beyond myself.

BETTERING ONESELF BY VALUING ANOTHER

If a sorority is a sisterhood composed of women who are family by choice, women who can relate to one another and share ideals and goals while supporting the individual qualities that give their chapter a unique vibe, can members of other sororities be considered like-minded cousins? Nothing can come between the lasting bonds of a small, tight-knit unit and its personal history; that nucleus is special in itself. However, belonging to a larger, loosely connected family rooted in similar notions of sisterhood can transform what began as girl power into a massive women's movement generating a greater impact on the world.

A REALLY BIG WORLD

Let's face it. The real world is big. It's beautiful, but that beauty can be shrouded by tough times. It can be scary. Sometimes we're only pretending to be strong until a friendly face kindly reminds us where we came from. Real life isn't nearly as scripted as sorority recruitment or core curriculum schedules. It's not as predictable as a college professor and his corduroy blazer. There's a certain naive confidence that college students carry around in their backpacks, unaware of the level of testing that exists beyond the walls of their institution. Not that college students aren't ready for the real world; it's just that a college diploma is hardly an answer key to life's real tests. Growing up can be a steady adjustment or a shock to the system, depending on the day. A sorority creed can be the lullaby that comforts a girl into believing she can handle all of it.

LASTING BONDS IN SISTERHOOD

We might not know much about a person other than feeling like we have something in common. Sometimes that commonality is a school, state, or, if a girl is lucky, sorority. While individual sorority stories are sacred, the extended connection to alumnae and even women from other sororities is also important. Some stories are acceptable to be shared with members outside the fraternity—not the sacred parts like the ritual or the initiation—but the good stuff, like the time you lost your keys and made everyone in your chapter house search for them, or when you could barely walk home in heels after a night of dancing, or when you sat on the front porch with your sisters to share a philosophical discussion about the importance of sparkly headbands. Funny memories give sorority girls something to talk about. We aren't perfect; we strive to become better by reflecting on the silliness and style of our former selves.

INSPIRED BY COMPETITION

A friendly-faced person might not know the details of your spunk or sass as a college girl, but she might be able to offer a connection that shows she can relate. Relating to others is the ultimate stress reducer. It's the same as hardworking adults sharing stories about their scars or comparing how tired they feel every day. We feel inspired by competition. If we have a bad day, but someone else has a worse day, it helps put our misfortunes into perspective. Suddenly we feel more capable of handling our own stuff, and more inspired to help others handle their stuff. It also helps us laugh about how life can be a big pain in the rear.

A FAMILY CONNECTION

Seeing another sorority girl out in the open is refreshing. It's an extension of that college safety net. It's like going on vacation to another country and meeting someone who's from your home state or country of origin. Immediately you have a bond. You might not be from the same town, but you are instantly linked by a greater chain, and suddenly you have a new best friend for the rest of the trip. While sororities have wonderful alumnae groups that keep girls connected beyond college, being able to share a sisterhood with sisters whose allegiance lies with other organizations is an olive branch from a larger family tree. Everyone has that one weird cousin—or maybe you are that weird cousin! Either way, friendly competition among distant relatives is a nice way to protect, promote, and celebrate the family name. In this case, that family crest is the larger umbrella of sorority sisterhood.

SHARING VALUES

While each sorority is unique, many are grounded in the same truths and ideals, even if they are described by different adjectives. Each sorority is special in its own right, and while each organization has its own finesse and original way of suggesting its principles—be they told in creed, purpose, or even a symphony—many of the values these girls stand for share a common thread.

AN ARMY OF SUPPORT

In 1922, Alpha Omicron Pi founder Stella Perry said, "What can we say to our children on Founders' Day but to pray that they may love one another as we love them, and bless the world with the love they have tested in the laboratory of our sisterhood?" With each sorority maintaining a commitment to bettering its local community and seeking out ways to influence its own philanthropic goals, it's hard to imagine what a map of the world would look like without sororities doing their part to leave a positive imprint on it. Footprints scatter through history, leading current sorority members down a path to the past and offering a bridge to a hopeful future. The millions of dollars donated through fund-raisers and group efforts, the countless hours dedicated to serving others, and the limitless volunteer work—all these positives add up to a lot of love. While NPC is structured as a friendly competition between sororities striving to be the best of the bunch, it's hard not to notice the grand similarities these life-changing organizations share in their members' hearts and souls. Every sorority has it written somewhere in their creed, or their ritual, or their symphony, a promise and a pledge to become the greatest version of oneself while honoring the humility of finding focus in helping others. Chi Omega's beautiful symphony, written in 1904 by Ethel Switzer Howard, Xi Chapter, is a shining example of the motivation that girls find in their sorority, "… to work earnestly, to speak kindly, to act sincerely, to choose thoughtfully that course which occasion and conscience demand; to be womanly always; to be discouraged never." Life's challenges are no match for the camaraderie found between these uplifting lines.

Crafting Tip

INSPIRATIONAL QUOTES

Sororities are all about inspiration. Why not keep that glow in your grown-up life by printing out your favorite line from your creed or symphony and putting it in a frame? If you're crafty, you could paint a canvas or a wooden plaque. If you're busy, print that paper out on your office's dime and slap it in your favorite dainty frame! All those crafty sorority picture frames might seem like a big waste of wood, so why not put all your printed pictures in a scrapbook, then repaint your wooden frames to give as gifts to your nieces and BFFs? You might be known as the tchotchke queen, but you can wear your crown with pride knowing you recycled the goods to someone else, thereby keeping the legacy of knickknacks alive and inspiring more girls to find creative ways to regift!

Chapter Four

THE LANGUAGE OF FRIENDSHIP

A young woman's commitment to her sorority begins at an impressionable age. The sisterhood she finds in fellow members is rooted in a shared spirit and hope to shape members into their best selves. Sorry for the cheese, but sororities can be the sunshine that helps their members grow! Sororities have traditions, rituals and symbols, just like sorority flowers, which represent personal messages and meanings. It turns out that flowers themselves also have their own girly language grown from centuries of myth and tradition. Interestingly enough, sophisticated women have always had a particular way of communicating with one another. Back in Victorian times, bouquets were used as a silent microphone for a fancy girl to nonverbally clear her throat and get some stuff off her chest. Upper class people were apparently so bored that they decided to create an entire encrypted language using flowers as pawns in a weird communicative game of glory chess. Sending ravens and owls as messengers was never really a thing, but giving flowers used to be. Each flower had its own meaning, and none of the real housewives of old towns needed a secret decoder ring to decipher their earthly deliveries—they had flower dictionaries instead! Floriography, or the language of flowers, was the handcrafted, unspoken, unwritten messaging system of the Victorian era. While sororities may or may not have researched the "dictionary" meaning behind their sorority flower choices, there's no harm in stopping to smell the roses to see what they are all about.

PASTE IN A KEEPSAKE
FROM YOUR FAVORITE
SORORITY TRADITION OR RITUAL

The Language of Friendship

Our sorority flower is:

_____

_____

_____

_____

My sisters help me grow by:

_____

_____

_____

_____

We dream of becoming:

_____

_____

_____

_____

When I first met my sisters, I thought:

_____

_____

_____

_____

_____

My sisters inspire me to:

_____

_____

_____

_____

_____

I hope that:

_____

_____

_____

_____

_____

The Language of Women

Every sorority girl had that one sorority sister whose voice went up a few decibels when talking about the sorority. It was like a special language, a flare of an accent, an intense, innate vocal switch that went off when a dire sorority situation needed to be taken seriously. It might have happened at a chapter meeting, or maybe you overheard your sister talking on the phone behind a closed door. Usually, the information wasn't that serious, seriously speaking. In sorority terms, it might have felt that way, like maybe a few girls casually sat on a glass coffee table at a formal dance and it shattered into a million pieces, leaving your executive officers up glitter creek with all the chapter's money blown on balloons and the disgruntled venue's representative asking everybody to pay up. Sometimes sorority sisters yell at each other—that's what family does. Don't be too hard on your sorority friends that sported the sorority phone voice; that specific articulation and hand flaring fueled their tough cookie spirit with seeds of real world character that helped them sprout into cunning career women!

CREATIVE MESSAGING

Back in the nineties, a sorority girl might have just slipped her sister a note under the door if they needed to talk. Today, we worry about a text message being misunderstood, emails being misconstrued, an unflattering facial expression taking hold of a misinterpretation of our mood before we've ingested twelve cups of coffee. Plus, we read into acronyms like it's some kind of warfare. "K." What does that mean? Is she mad? "It's fine." Is it fine? Is it *really*? Sorority girls today may band together to decipher the meaning of their chapter president's short and sweet responses. Victorian chicks didn't have technology and reality television, so presumably, they needed to spice up their neighborhood gossip somehow. Who could blame them for not wanting to actually verbalize their feelings? They didn't have the luxury of deciphering text messages for hours on end. What would any of us be doing if we didn't agonize over our email grammar and emoji choices? How would we get out of having to actually call someone or see them face to face to tell them how we feel? Flowers—we'd probably be sending everyone flowers.

THE MEANING OF FLOWERS

Wouldn't it be cool to present a message to someone without having to write it down or visualize it in emoji form? In sorority land, flowers are a piece of tradition, history, and friendship. Since sororities are foundations upon which college girls can blossom into strong women, flowers can be a symbol of personal growth and shared culture. No flower is the wrong flower in this language, and all of them symbolize a shared love of a dear sorority.

DECODING FLOWERS

In Victorian life, flower dictionaries were more like coffee-table crossword puzzles, not methods of plotting vengeance. It's funny to think about, though. This is what happens to women when they don't have the option of joining a sorority. They get bored and start gardening—aggressively. Their nonverbal messages took the form of bouquets that might have been in the running for mean girl marketing. "I don't like you—here are some flowers that say that." Today we would just post something to social media and forget about it. Flower arranging seems like a lot of work for someone you aren't that fond of, and all that gardening and flower arranging had to have been exhausting.

UNEXPECTED SYMBOLS

Let's talk flowers and the modern chicks that gush over the surprise of their delivery. What well-rounded woman doesn't love an unexpected floral arrangement? As long as it's not at her own funeral, a girl is probably elated. Some flowers have potent fragrances that could be tied to a sensitive memory, and that's understandable, but it's not a lily's fault for being a popular funeral accomplice. Lilies are there to symbolize something hopeful and innocent, so give them a break! If it's a lily of the valley, kindly don't give them a break, they're epically poisonous. They are beautiful, though, and symbolize a return of happiness. So long as you don't eat them. In celebration, sympathy, friendship, or love, a floral gift has kind intentions. Does it really matter exactly which types of flowers make up the bouquet? To Victorians, it did, and to sorority girls, certain types of flowers might conjure fond feelings of their college glory days!

The Language of Women

Our sorority flower makes me think about:

_____
_____
_____
_____
_____

Our sorority helped me get better at:

_____
_____
_____
_____
_____

If I could go back in time, I would:

_____
_____
_____
_____
_____

I get sentimental when I think about:

_____

_____

_____

_____

_____

If my sisters were flowers, they would be:

_____

_____

_____

_____

I wish our flower was:

_____

_____

_____

_____

_____

Stories of Growth

Growth. Every hurdle friends clear together is a step toward a tighter bond. While sorority sisters grow together, the culture of sororities themselves continues to grow and evolve with time. While it's enlightening to recall stories about how flowers first bloomed, their mythological roots are only the beginning of their place on Earth. Today, flowers have grown to become symbols that are both personally and widely accepted. Each sorority has its own reason for choosing its flower—such reasons are likely not tied to these myths, but rather the tradition of the sorority and the start of its own story in the history of female friendship and sisterly support.

FRIENDSHIP FILLERS

Today, it's pretty common knowledge that yellow flowers mean friendship. Most every girl who's had a crush on someone knows that receiving a bouquet of yellow bulbs is an Einstein moment suggesting that the relationship only lights up in the friend zone. That's great for platonic friends, but not so great if a girl is looking for some kind of sign that her crush more than likes her—that he, like, *like-likes* her. Duh. If a guy likes a girl and buys her a bouquet of red roses symbolizing love and she isn't interested, the girl might suggest they are beautiful, but a shade of yellow would have been nice, too. A yellow carnation could mean disdain, disappointment, or rejection. *Ouch.* Some teachers might think about filling a detention hall with them. Whereas a yellow rose could mean infidelity to one lady, someone else might see friendship and joy. It's all about perspective.

CARNATIONS

Perhaps carnations are a popular sorority flower because their history dates back to ancient Rome and Greece where they were used as ceremonial crowns. There's much speculation (and confusion) surrounding the origin of the word carnation. Some think it might stem from a mispronunciation of the term "coronation" or the act of crowning. It's been linked to the Roman term *corona*, which means crown or garland. Since the original color of the flower is a delicate pink, it's also been said that carnation comes from words that mean flesh, such as the Latin *caro* or the Greek *carnis*. Technically, these colorful cloves are called Dianthus Caryophyllus (try saying that three times fast). Did it get a nickname because it's too ridiculous to pronounce over the phone while ordering a bouquet from the local florist? There's no proof of such a claim anywhere, just an obvious speculation here. Anyway, some Greek flower dude (also known simply as a botanist) was first to call this work of art "Dianthus," meaning divine flower, flower of the gods. In modern times, it's one of the more affordable options at the flower shop, and if that's not a divine quality to love, what is?

A COLORFUL COLLECTION

The fun thing about carnations is that they come in a variety of shades and each one has its own meaning and symbolism, sort of like sororities! The pink carnation is indicative of a women's lasting, undying love. A suggestion of what's never to be forgotten, a divine sisterhood. Word has it that people believe pink carnations first graced the Earth from the tears of the Virgin Mary—a mother's devotion. It's thought that a light red carnation is a symbol of admiration, while a deeper red is indicative of an aching heart. No, not a broken one, just one that's so full of love, so divine, it aches to be human. *Sigh.* It does ache to be human. Purple carnations represent capriciousness and unpredictability but can also be presented in the hindsight of such behavior as an apology. White carnations are pure, true, sweet, and delicate; some say they are even representative of good luck, so maybe pack a few in your purse or sport a corsage the next time you plan on taking a trip to the casino with the girls. Nobody ever really said they worked that way, but nobody ever really said they didn't. Smelling good while carrying good vibes is a win-win.

THE IRIS

Speaking of flowers sending messages, the iris earned its name from an epic go-between, go-to gal. The ancient Greek goddess, Iris, was a messenger to the gods who apparently used a rainbow as a bridge to connect heaven and Earth. Iris, indeed, is the Greek word for rainbow. While being named after such a force makes the iris flower an epic representation of girl power and glory, it's also kind of akin to men. The more than 200 varieties found on the planet are typically divided into two groups: the bearded and the unbearded. Bearded irises are more like the dudes that can't really grow a beard, but try to anyway, and the end result of these bearded irises are far more impressive. They look like they have a tiny little beard because the "falls," or lower petals that drop down, are kind of fuzzy. Unbearded irises are naturally clean shaven with zero fuzzies. (If only our legs could work that way.) Purple irises indicate complimentary wisdom, blue ones are symbols of hope, white ones suggest something pure (shocker), and yellow ones are symbols of ... passion! Points for yellow! A yellow iris is much nicer than a disappointing yellow carnation. It's hard not to feel bad for the yellow carnation; whoever gave it such a disappointing connotation must have been disappointed by the giver, not the gift. If you like yellow carnations, let them mean sunshine, or whatever you want instead. Somebody needs to throw the yellow carnation a bone.

LILY OF THE VALLEY

Even the phrase lily of the valley sounds warm and hopeful, slightly whimsical. Could it be imagined that lilies of the valley are prominent in the enchanted forests where unicorns are an actual species? One can only hope, but no current scientific research suggests it. Truly, lilies of the valley symbolize a return to happiness. They are also called Our Lady's Tears and May Bells. These lovely flowers representing purity of heart, humility, and tears of the Virgin Mary reach their pinnacle form in the month of May to welcome in the happiness of the summer months. It's thought that the drooping flowers of lily of the valley are representative of the tears Mary cried at the crucifixion of Jesus Christ. In Victorian times, chicks would apparently frolic off into the woods on lily picnics—surrounding a poisonous plant? Perhaps those flower dictionaries *were* more than crossword time killers.

THOUGHTFUL PICKING

Pansies come from the French term, *pensée*, meaning thought. They are symbols that express a yearning for someone to keep another in their thoughts. The Victorians believed that pansies embodied the feminine qualities of a girl's heart: compassion, tenderness, and thoughtfulness. Next time someone tries to use the term pansy in a derogatory sense, tell them their insensitivity is a compliment for being sensitive and caring. So thanks!

THINKING ABOUT TAKING SWIM LESSONS

Forget-me-not flowers represent exactly what they seem to, an inherent desire to be loyal to a lasting promise, to not forget, and to love always. Simply, these pretty blue petals are memorable for their uncomplicated expression of love. Their backstory comes from a German folk tale about a couple walking alongside a riverbank. The bride-to-be is oohing and aahing over a bunch of flowers near the edge, and her clumsy but good-intentioned future husband takes a plunge while trying to pick them for her. As he gets lost downstream, he throws the bouquet at his beloved and yells (in German), "Forget me not!" A glass-is-half-full person has to imagine the groom had coincidentally been taking swimming lessons leading up to the wedding, and due to these trainings he was able to casually wade his way to shore to embrace his fiancée. They told the story at their rehearsal dinner while everyone laughed because the bridegroom was dripping wet. That's how it must have went down—not with him drowning or anything. Who doesn't love a happy ending?

THE ROSE

Writing history wouldn't be complete without roses. Roses in beds, roses on floors, roses at celebrations, and roses in wars. Roses at funerals and roses to fight feeling dead after a night—of drinking. There are many stories of roses in the realm of ancient Greeks and Romans, perhaps the most important takeaway being that Romans used to drop rose petals into their wine because they thought the flower could thwart drunkenness. A love-infused hangover-curing cocktail! You're welcome.

QUEEN OF FLOWERS

In Greek mythology, Chloris is the goddess of flowers. When she came upon the lifeless body of a nymph in the forest, she didn't just keep walking. She called upon some other gods to do a good deed, and they gave the dead nymph a new life as a blooming flower. How cute.

MORE CRYING

Another flower born from the tears of a woman. *Sigh*. If only that trick worked today, we'd stop crying over stupid stuff—or start crying over everything and use it as a fancy party trick. This time it's the ancient Greeks and their goddess of love, Aphrodite, crying over her ill-fated beau, Adonis. First of all, white roses were already around at this point because they were created when Aphrodite was born. There's this whole thing about the father of the sky, Ouranos, and him being tragically castrated and falling into the sea, then suddenly Aphrodite being born and white roses rising up everywhere out of sea foam. Actually, sounds pretty badass. Time to fast-forward to roses becoming red. There's a few versions involving Aphrodite, one regarding Ares, the god of war. Apparently, he was jealous of Adonis so he decided to morph into a wild boar and attack him. Ancient era 'roid rage?

Aphrodite learned of this ridiculous crime show activity and went to help Adonis, except she cut herself on a thorn bush, splattering blood on the pure white petals and creating red roses in the process. (At least she wasn't wearing white pants at the time.) Another version has Aphrodite crying over Adonis's dead, bloody body. Her tears mixed with his blood and red roses were born. It's kind of a morbid story, but sometimes love can be messy?

SHH … IT'S A SECRET

The Romans liked to call Aphrodite "Venus," kind of like a stage name for her world tour. Apparently, her son, Cupid, offered the god of silence a rose as a bribing tool because Venus was out roaming around with dudes and Cupid wanted to brush those antics under the carpet (he couldn't bear to hear any more your mama jokes), so it's said that roses have been tied to secrecy ever since. In the Middle Ages, roses hung from ceilings of meeting rooms as a universal signifier of secrecy. It was understood that everything discussed under the roses was done in confidence and wouldn't be shared elsewhere. Roses above were the ancient equivalent of a 1990s pinky swear or a modern-day sorority handshake.

A PASSIONATE SET OF PETALS

Red roses are symbolic of love and romance; everyone knows that. Pink roses show offerings of gratitude, grace, and happiness. Orange roses are passionate and enthusiastic, except when people refer to them as gingers. Yellow roses mean friendship, and, yes, white roses represent pure innocence.

THE VIOLET

Roman mythology suggests that Venus created blue violets out of rage. Oops. One day, she asked her son, Cupid, to compare her to a bunch of girls. She asked who was prettier, her or the girls, as if Cupid was a magic mirror. Anyway, Cupid was quite the troublemaker and decided to tell his mom that the girls were better looking. Venus became upset, obviously, so her only option was to go and beat the crap out of those other girls until they turned blue. Seems excessive, but Cupid should have just been a mama's boy and he could have saved these girls from all that bruising. Anyway, nothing was left to do at the end except cover her tracks and turn those girls into flowers. Cupid, such a menace with that arrow. Could that be why violets symbolize modesty and humility? There's also the other story about Apollo and the hots he had for Ia, the daughter of Midas. Apollo was like a modern-day bro-dude that wouldn't take no for an answer, so a goddess named Diana turned Ia into a violet to save her from being maimed by Apollo's inability to read what a girl wants (or clearly doesn't want). If it was a modern-day tale, Apollo would have been the one that was turned into a cactus and Ia would have gone on to do great things.

BUDDING FRIENDSHIPS

The cool thing about myths is that they could be rooted in truth; they were crafted so long ago, who really knows? It's like when one girl tells another girl something, and that girl tells another girl something, and none of it probably happened anyway. Does your sorority have its own story related to how your flower choice happened? Most sororities today are tied to these flowers: carnations, roses, violets, pansies, irises, lilies of the valley, and forget-me-nots. They are all beautiful in their own color and their own right. Today, sorority girls are not just reflecting on the myths and traditions that took shape and form in chapter houses over the course of a century, but continue to add branches to their sorority's development and growth.

With respect to truths rooted in the past, each chapter builds its own tale in a bigger book; that's what growth is all about. Women are constantly rewriting the future and repainting the picture, and women of the past gave us the creative tools. Being in a sorority is not about encouraging a girl to belong, it's about providing inspirational support to live a full life as a well-rounded individual fueled by seeds of the past, light of the present, and future seasons of new beginnings.

Crafting Tip

FLOWER POWER

It's easy to get caught up in our fast-paced world, but there's plenty of old-school ways to stay connected, and sometimes that nontech lifestyle is a breath of fresh air. Instead of texting your BFF on her birthday, why not mail her a token of your friendship or a simple, sweet greeting card? You could send her a bouquet of your sorority flowers! If you hope to have reminders of your old sorority friends at home, think about incorporating your sorority flower into your house decor. They don't have to be the real thing. Think about finding a cute box, watering can, birdcage, lantern, or vase that can house fake flower petals and bring back fond memories of your sisters. You can line a picture frame with flowers or create a hanging flower garland as a symbol of life's new beginnings without forgetting your college legacy.

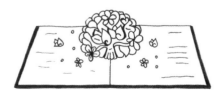

Chapter Five

INSPIRING A LIFETIME OF LEADERSHIP

The schoolyard insult "You play like a girl" is probably not something a boy wants to hear from his coach, father, or friend. It suggests that the boy's efforts are not up to the standards of a tough kid. It's as if playing like a girl means the boy is not a competitor. A deeper look at the efforts of sorority women might make a boy change his mind. Playing like a girl may not be such a bad idea, as girls have a proven ability to adapt to our surroundings and to the needs of those around us. We can be cunning and clever. We can read a room and comprehend our place in it. Toughness should not be the interchangeable adjective for masculine. Toughness can come from within—it's like a stubborn spirit—a dire hope to better the world around us, a decision made after deep thoughts of how to forge a path of leadership. Leading the way doesn't necessarily mean being in charge of others, it means being in charge of oneself while understanding the influence we have on others. Sorority women have become game-changers in every arena there is to succeed, and they're not just succeeding, they're trailblazing and forging pathways for future ambitious women to follow in their footsteps. These success stories do not dictate, but rather encourage young women to pave their own way to happiness and self-completion. Since the early days of sorority women, alumnae have been making strides for themselves, and females in general, in their respective fields. Sororities are not about recruiting girls that fit into a cookie-cutter image of a woman of the past. In fact, sorority life is founded on women that think outside the box and create their own place in the world as it evolves. It's about shaping female role models into who they want to be, not who others think they should be. That's a freedom that takes flight in sisterhood.

PASTE IN A KEEPSAKE OF YOU
AND YOUR ROLE MODEL

Inspiring a Lifetime of Leadership

Our recruitment parties were:

_____

_____

_____

_____

_____

We rocked at:

_____

_____

_____

_____

_____

Preference night was:

_____

_____

_____

_____

_____

My favorite theme was:

_____

_____

_____

_____

_____

Bid day was:

_____

_____

_____

_____

_____

We were always:

_____

_____

_____

_____

_____

Recruiting
Game-Changing Women

Any ancient peeps that were worried about women losing their finishing school status upon entering college should have been flies on the walls of today's sorority houses. Sure, they'd likely find some chaos, but they'd also see young women sharing clothes, ideas, recipes, pep talks, and textbooks. Sorority girls learn how to be good teammates as big and little sisters. They come to understand the importance of legacy, tradition, and confidentiality through initiation. Chapter meetings give them a glimpse of the corporate world, and social events provide a platform for them to craft a balance. Recruitment trains young women to be fierce, polite, and intelligent at networking and mingling under pressure. The hours of primping, prepping, and personality-training we sorority girls mastered during the days of glamming it up in leopard-print letters actually prepared us with a firsthand look at the future—and we are stronger because of it.

A REALITY CRAFTED IN RECRUITMENT

In the real world, men and women make snap judgments daily, from interviewing for jobs to skimming online dating sites. Being able to assess a person in a short amount of time by getting to know their story, observing their body language, and reading their reactions is a learned skill that is necessary to navigating the real world. Just as it's difficult becoming a college student with so many new challenges to conquer, finding a place as a postgrad adult can feel like a chaotic spiral into the unknown. It's easy to make snap judgments; the difficult part is making the best decision possible in situations that aren't always ideal. Sorority girls build their smiles, their voices, and their stamina during chapter events. Working women that once worked a room during sorority recruitment can take pride in walking tall. After all, the shiny pumps that reflect their paychecks have heels that click back to days of meeting, befriending, and inviting potential new members (PNMs) into a special group that dreams beyond dormitory walls. Sisterhood is not just a college thing—it's a lifelong bond structured to challenge, comfort, and keep well-intended women on their toes.

SEEKING STRENGTH TOGETHER

Sometimes the real world isn't fair. All a sorority girl can do is play the game by the rules, wear her letters on her heart, and hope that her college experience has given her the guts to assess any situation with a sincere and level head. Sometimes a person needs to make conversation with strangers. Sometimes a person doesn't jibe well with someone else. That's okay. Everyone doesn't have to belong everywhere. Not every job is the right one. Not every relationship lasts. Sometimes a PNM and a sorority might not be a match, even if the PNM thinks she could belong there. Receiving such disappointment sucks, but a girl isn't going to get called back from every job she applies to or every guy she dates. Just as a girl isn't always going to want to work at the company that offers her a role. It's a pick-and-choose world. Planting the seeds for thick skin early on helps a person develop the gumption to handle disappointment and conquer challenges through the highs and lows of life.

CAREER-READY CHICKS

The life skills that are budding at recruitment parties are abundant. Yes, being able to color-coordinate outfits with thirty other chicks at the same time is a feat fit for starring in a viral music video, but there are more important life lessons at hand. Sorority members band together to figure out how to market their best selves; these are the same self-promoting muscles chicks are going to need to flex when trying to prove themselves to potential employers. It's human to want to belong and to be liked by others; the stresses that come with finding a home on a college campus are a helpful introduction to the harshness of navigating a life after school. Luckily, many sororities set girls up to have lifelong bonds  as members of alumnae groups. Many sororities are connected through social media accounts today, but before that, Gamma Phi Beta had a *TranSISter* program that provided phone information of alumnae in every state. Alpha Phi's *Transitions* magazine, geared toward seniors and new graduates, was created to help girls through that tough period between college and the real world. For some, that change can seem like a scary teleportation to another universe. Having a support system can help a girl understand that her state of mind is totally normal no matter what she is feeling! It's not just about finding a home away from home in college, it's about finding an extended family and a link to your past—for life.

SORORITY LIFE COULD BE A SPORT

It's nice to become part of a support system that will remind a chick just how many people she has holding her up. It's not one girl against the world when the bonds of sisterhood are her buoy. The frat boys might be disappointed. It's not the boobs that float—it's the love and support. It's one girl and her sisters, working toward individual and team goals, chanting songs and making memories along the way. Not every sister is the same, and that's what makes a chapter house a family. There is nothing cultish about being in a sorority (right?). Sure, there are chants, candles, rituals, and initiations. But that doesn't make it weird. Sororities are more like sports teams—we have superstitions, songs, and handshakes. We celebrate wins and share losses—together. Girls learn how to be team players while seeking independence. Their walk alone is lit by friendship, a candle fueled by confidence, creativity, and charisma.

Recruiting Game-Changing Women

Initiation is:

_____

_____

_____

_____

_____

Ritual is:

_____

_____

_____

_____

I am inspired by:

_____

_____

_____

_____

_____

Our executive officers are:

_____

_____

_____

_____

_____

Chapter meetings are:

_____

_____

_____

_____

_____

Our sorority prepares us for life by:

_____

_____

_____

_____

_____

Game-Changing Sorority Girls

Nobody can presume to think that belonging to a sorority seals the fate of a promising young college student. Women can make a difference in many ways, in the home and the lives of their children, in the workplace and the lives of their coworkers, or in any way they find important. There are strong women out there that have done the impossible whether they own letters or not, but perhaps being exposed to other like-minded women at an impressionable time is exactly what a girl needs to spark her own energy toward something that could make a difference in her life. Could a sorority girl's potential be unlocked by a simple secret handshake or a sacred initiation ritual? Every story is different, but it's not a total stretch to wonder if accomplished women trace their successful wings back to the roots of their sorority days.

INSPIRATION FOR ALL FIELDS

Sororities formed back when women didn't have much of a voice on college campuses; now we can't stop talking and sharing information! For some former sorority women, it's their job to jabber. There are many women in the news and entertainment business that were once members of sororities, and some have done their share to carve women a place in these industries. Notable Sigma Delta Tau alum Marilyn Salenger was the first female to solo anchor a newscast. She went on to create the first all-women's television news program in the United States. Another SDT alum, Sherry Lansing, was the first woman to head a Hollywood studio. She was previously the CEO of Paramount Pictures. Joan Cooeny was a member of Kappa Alpha Theta that went on to found Children's Television Workshop in 1964, creating *Sesame Street* and putting a positive stamp on everyone's childhood. Soap opera lovers that can't get enough sap in their late mornings can thank Phi Sigma Sigma alum Irna Phillips for creating *Guiding Light*, *As the World Turns*, *Days of our Lives,* and *Another World*. There are plenty of sorority women creating better worlds in the arts and entertainment industry, the news business, politics, sports, science, education, and just about every other branch of life that exists. If a branch they imagine isn't quite there yet, a sorority woman might be the type to take the leap and build her landing midflight. These confident chicks welcome challenge and are inspired by it.

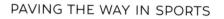

PAVING THE WAY IN SPORTS

Before Margaret Unnewehr-Schott became president of the Cincinnati Reds, she was a Theta Phi Alpha sorority girl. Susan Sylvester Hutchison was an Alpha Delta Pi that became Hawaii's first female sportscaster, Claire Waters Ferguson was an Alpha Phi that became the first female president of the US Figure Skating Association, and Eleanor Logan was a Kappa Kappa Gamma that became the first American rower to win a gold medal in three consecutive Olympics. The first female football manager in the NCAA, Elaine Reckard Lenvo, coached the Georgia Tech Yellow Jackets and was formerly a member of Alpha Delta Pi. Fay Burnett was a member of Sigma Kappa that became the first nutritionist for Weight Watchers International; she wrote the first maintenance plan. Tatiana McFadden was a Phi Sigma Sigma that went on to medal in the Paralympics seventeen times, and Alpha Chi Omega alumna Julie Brown was a distance runner that won the 1975 World Cross Country Championship and competed in the marathon in the 1984 Olympics. The distance sorority women have traveled, the miles they have added to the elevation of a woman's road to achievement, the number of times they have planted the seeds for equality—it's all astounding. It's impossible to highlight all the women that have left a mark on the lives of others, but it's inspiring to reflect on some of the names that are stitched in each sorority's claim to fame.

PLAYING THE BEST ROLE

Alpha Sigma Alpha alum and high school teacher Freida Riley was known for the work she did with her students, Homer Hickam and the Rocket Boys. The feature film *October Sky* is based on Riley's inspirational teachings, and actress Laura Dern plays Riley on the big screen. Leigh Anne Tuohy, a former Kappa Delta girl who was portrayed on the silver screen by Academy Award-winning actress Sandra Bullock, is the woman whose family took in high school football player Michael Oher. Their heartwarming, hometown fairy tale became Hollywood's *The Blind Side*. Gamma Phi Beta sisters and identical biological siblings, Joan Knoerzer Hackett and Jane Knoerzer Schwartz, were the original Doublemint Twins. Before Anne Turner Cook became a member of Pi Beta Phi, she started a tradition as the original Gerber baby. Before Betty White was a *Golden Girl*, she was a member of the girls of Alpha Gamma Delta. *To Kill a Mockingbird* author Harper Lee was a member of Chi Omega.

COMBINING INGREDIENTS FOR A BALANCED LIFE

Marjorie Husted was a Kappa Alpha Theta that went on to mold and craft the Betty Crocker brand into a successful empire through writing and performing radio broadcasts, along with becoming the director of the Betty Crocker Homemaking Service in 1929. Meanwhile, Delta Zeta alumna Mercedes Bates became the first female corporate officer of General Mills Foods as the vice president of the Betty Crocker division in 1966. People often referred to Bates as Betty Crocker because of her role at the company. So at least two former sorority women embodied the essence of the renowned homemaking queen whose recipes we all drool over.

SHOOTING FOR THE STARS

These girls aimed high. When Sigma Kappa alum Dr. Rhea Seddon went to space, her sorority badge was in tow. Judith Resnik was a member of Alpha Epsilon Phi and the first Jewish American to travel to space; she was a NASA astronaut that tragically perished in the Space Shuttle Challenger disaster. Laurel Clark was a member of Gamma Phi Beta; she was killed when the Columbia space shuttle disintegrated upon reentering the Earth's atmosphere. Though both life stories ended on a sad note, both women are celebrated and their accomplishments will continue to inspire young girls to dream among the clouds. As will Alpha Xi Delta alumna Jan Davis, who went to space with her husband! Talk about finding love and a purpose. The couple was the first married pair to travel to space together. Then there was NASA astronaut Susan J. Helms, the first woman to live on an international space station, and a Chi Omega alum. Not to forget Bonnie Dunbar, a former member of Kappa Delta that was inducted into the US Astronaut Hall of Fame and Women in Technology Hall of Fame. Mareta West was the first female astrogeologist. She chose the site for the first manned lunar landing and was a member of Kappa Kappa Gamma in college. And let's not discount the high flyers that stayed within Earth's atmosphere, like Geraldine "Jerrie" Fredritz Mock. She didn't just have a badass name, she was a badass pilot. She married a pilot, too, and he supported her goal of becoming the first woman to successfully fly solo around the world in 1964!

EARNING RESPECT IN THEIR RESPECTIVE FIELDS

Brigadeer General Margaret A. Brewer was the first woman general of the United States Marine Corps and a former member of Zeta Tau Alpha. Tova Wiley was a Phi Mu that became the first woman to hold the rank of commander in the US Navy; she earned the legion of merit award. Kappa Delta alum Claudia Kennedy was the US Army's first three-star general. Mimi Blackburn Drew was a member of Alpha Xi Delta; she went on to become the first female rear admiral in the US Navy. Alpha Epsilon Phi alum Judith Hirschfield was the first woman to teach math at Harvard University. Sarah Tilman Hughes, a Delta Gamma, was the first female federal judge and the first woman to swear in a United States president (Lyndon B. Johnson). The first woman to head an Ivy League law school (Barbara Aronstein Black) and first female president of an Ivy League university (Judith Redin) were both members of Delta Phi Epsilon. The president and CEO of White Castle (Elizabeth Ingram) was a member of Delta Gamma, and Tri Delta alum Sara Blakely wasn't just about keeping sorority traditions secretly tucked away; she founded the women's shapewear brand *Spanx*, boosting the social confidence of millions of women.

A LONG LIST OF ACCOMPLISHED SORORITY WOMEN

The first American woman to win the Nobel prize in literature was a Kappa Delta alumna named Pearl Sydenstricker Buck. Susan Shannon Engeleiter, a former member of Delta Gamma, was the first woman to head the Small Business Administration. The first woman to receive a PhD in psychology, Margaret Floy Washburn, was a former member of Kappa Alpha Theta. Dr. Gladys Henry Dick codiscovered the Dick test for scarlet fever and the antitoxin used in the treatment of scarlet fever. She was a member of Pi Beta Phi, as was Kathryn Lyle Stephenson, MD, the first board-certified female plastic surgeon in the United States. The first woman to earn an electrical engineering degree from MIT was Edith Clarke, a Kappa Kappa Gamma. Some of the country's first female mayors and governors wore sorority letters in college. Letters, merit, and accomplishment mean something to sorority alumnae, that's for sure.

REDEFINING SUCCESS

From CIA spies to elected government officials, to Olympians and CEOs of Fortune 500 companies, it seems any list of notable alumnae is going to be an abbreviated one. That's because every woman has her own story and definition of what is notable in her own life after college. Not every name finds itself on any given assessment of what society finds impressive. Sorority women have broken down barriers and built bridges between them by redefining what it means to be a successful, well-balanced woman. Ultimately, being accomplished means any number of things in any field. Being a good

mother, daughter, sister, and friend is one of life's greatest achievements. Being able to find a balance between child-bearer and career-minded homemaker is a complicated dance. Luckily, sorority women laid the foundation for us to choreograph our own stories. The moments we share, the dances, the talks, the tests of friendship, these chapters are our own. The steps we take after graduation are up to us, but we can find gratitude in knowing we can find our way back to our old selves any time we need. The laughs, the tears, the lessons, and the years are forever embedded into our own sorority storybook that will continue to stay sacred as we grow old. We may be geographically apart, but sisters that share a history will always be young together, as our souls and hearts fondly recall the college glory days that gave us insight into the future we live now.

Shh! It's a Secret

Time to spill the beans! Share a special memory, inside joke, or moment that's close to your heart. Don't worry, these lines won't leave a digital footprint. Let your creativity shine and write or draw what's on your mind—the old-fashioned way!

NOW, PASTE IN YOUR
FAVORITE SORORITY MEMORIES!

NOW, PASTE IN YOUR
FAVORITE SORORITY MEMORIES!

NOW, PASTE IN YOUR
FAVORITE SORORITY MEMORIES!

NOW, PASTE IN YOUR
FAVORITE SORORITY MEMORIES!

NOW, PASTE IN YOUR
FAVORITE SORORITY MEMORIES!

NOW, PASTE IN YOUR
FAVORITE SORORITY MEMORIES!

About the Author

Melanie J. Pellowski attended college in New Brunswick, New Jersey, the same city where the doctor yelled, "It's a cheerleader!" when she was born to Michael and Judith Pellowski on June 14, 1983. The daughter of a former Rutgers football captain and his high school sweetheart, Melanie is the only girl among three brothers and preferred to take up tap dancing and three other sports instead: cross country, basketball, and softball.

A team mentality and life shaped by sports had Melanie searching for camaraderie and sisterhood as a college student. She became a member of Alpha Chi Omega's Theta Tau chapter at Rutgers University in 2002 and was elected VP of recruitment in her senior year.

Melanie graduated Phi Beta Kappa from Douglass College, Rutgers University in 2005 with a major in American studies and minors in mathematics and theatre arts. She went on to earn a master's degree in journalism from Boston University in 2008. The lasting bonds she formed with her Alpha Chi sisters are the inspiration for this book, and some of those friends even stood by her as bridesmaids when she married the love of her life in August 2017.

Melanie writes under her maiden name. She and her husband, Nick, happily reside in Hunterdon County, New Jersey.

Acknowledgments

This book would not have been possible without the family I was born into and the family I made through love and friendship.

This project first came to mind when I became a member of Alpha Chi Omega at Rutgers University back in 2002, followed by my role as recruitment chair my senior year. The sisters that were a part of Alpha Chi at that time were surely a special, well-rounded bunch. Thank you to them for being kooky, caring, and fun. Had they not welcomed me in when I was having doubts as a new member, my college experience and life since then would not have been the same.

Thank you, Douglass College, for training me and preparing me to believe that lifelong education matters, and for introducing me to some of my best girlfriends as a hopeful college freshman.

Thank you to the Rutgers professors that had a sense of humor about my writing, especially in the American Studies department.

Thank you, Boston University, for helping me grow.

Thank you to all the sororities and female fraternities that have provided girls with an inspiring social, intellectual, and giving network of like-minded women. I am especially grateful to Alpha Phi's Linda Kahangi, Alpha Omicron Pi's Mariellen Sasseen, Kappa Alpha Theta's Liz Rinck, Chi Omega's Leslie Herington, and Alpha Xi Delta's Lauren Felts for their positive vibes, participation, and feedback.

Thank you to my father, Michael, for his patience, support, and sense of humor while I deliberated with him over the phone about whether or not I should join a sorority.

Thank you to my mother, Judy, for encouraging me to pursue my goals while showing me how to be kind and visiting me when I needed a hug.

Thank you to my brothers, Morgan, Matthew, and Martin, for teaching me to be a strong and ambitious team player.

Thank you to my sisters-in-law, Anastasia, Jenny, and Jackie, and my dear nonsorority friends that became like family: Michelle, Jenny, Caitlin, and Christy.

Thank you to my sorority sisters, especially P-Dawg, Jeanette, Alla, Shari, Mary, Eileen, Carly, Adrienne, Casey, Corrin, Shira, Sabrina, and Rina for all the memories and good times.

 Thank you to my husband, Nick, for all your love and support.

 Finally, I must extend a huge thank you to Nicole Mele and Skyhorse Publishing for believing in girl power and making all of this possible.

Bibliography

"19th Amendment." *History*. www.history.com/topics/womens-history/19th-amendment. Accessed January 2018.

Alpha Chi Omega: Real. Strong. Women. Alpha Chi Omega Fraternity, 2018, www.alphachiomega.org/. Accessed January 2018.

AlphachiomegaHQ. "Alpha Chi Omega – The Early Years (Part 1). https://youtu.be/HopHNwz9BSU. Online video clip. YouTube. YouTube, September 29, 2010. January 2018.

AlphachiomegaHQ. "Alpha Chi Omega – The Early Years (Part 2). https://youtu.be/SaliiPUB_Sk. Online video clip. YouTube. YouTube, September 29, 2010. January 2018.

Alpha Delta Pi: First. Finest. Forever. Since 1851. Alpha Delta Pi Sorority, 2018, www.alphadeltapi.org/. Accessed January 2018.

Alpha Epsilon Phi. Alpha Epsilon Phi Sorority, www.aephi.org. Accessed January 2018.

Alpha Gamma Delta: Live with Purpose. Alpha Gamma Delta Fraternity, 2018, www.alphagammadelta.org. Accessed January 2018.

Alpha Omicron Pi: Inspire Ambition. Alpha Omicron Pi International Fraternity, 2018, www.alphaomicronpi.org. Accessed January 2018.

Alpha Phi International. Alpha Phi Fraternity, 2017, www.alphaphi.org. Accessed January 2018.

Alpha Sigma Alpha: Developing Women of Poise and Purpose. Alpha Sigma Alpha Sorority, 2018, www.alphasigmaalpha.org. Accessed January 2018.

Alpha Sigma Tau: Defining Excellence. Alpha Sigma Tau Sorority, 2018, www.alphasigmatau.org. Accessed January 2018.

Alpha Xi Delta: Realize your Potential. Alpha Xi Delta Fraternity, 2018, www.alphaxidelta.org. Accessed January 2018.

Baird's Manual of American College Fraternities, Volume 9, Part 1920. G. Banta Company, 1920.

Barcelona, Leanna. "Past to Present: Rush to Recruitment." *Student Life and Culture Archives at the University of Illinois Archives*, 27 Aug. 2015. Accessed January 2018.

Becque, Fran. *Fraternity History & More*. www.franbecque.com/. Accessed January 2018.

Bonzo, Hannah. "History of Greek Life in Higher Education." *Rehoboth Journal*, 16 Oct. 2014, www.rehobothjournal.org/history-of-greek-life/. Accessed January 2018.

Brown, Kyle. "The Differences Between Fraternity and Sorority Rush. *Odyssey*. 14 Sept. 2015. www.theodysseyonline.com/differences-between-fraternity-sorority-rush. Accessed January 2018.

Chi Omega Fraternity: Sisters on Purpose. Chi Omega Fraternity, www.chiomega.com. Accessed January 2018.

Delta Gamma Fraternity. Delta Gamma Fraternity, www.deltagamma.org. Accessed January 2018.

Delta Phi Epsilon: Esse Quam Videri. Delta Phi Epsilon Sorority, 2016, www.dphie.org. Accessed January 2018.

Delta Zeta: Truly. Delta Zeta Sorority, www.deltazeta.org. Accessed January 2018.

"Flowers & History." *The Flower Expert: Guide on Flowers & Gardening*, www.theflowerexpert.com/content/miscellaneous/flowers-and-history. Accessed January 2018.

"Flowers and their Meaning." *Teleflora*, www.teleflora.com/meaning-of-flowers#Iris. Accessed January 2018.

"Flowers and their Meanings." *Flower Meaning*, www.flowermeaning.com. Accessed January 2018.

"Flower Meaning: The Language of Flowers." *The Old Farmer's Almanac*, www.almanac.com/content/flower-meanings-language-flowers. Accessed January 2018.

"Flower Meanings: The Meaning of Different Flowers." *ProFlowers*, 18 Jan. 2017, www.proflowers.com/blog/flower-meanings. Accessed January 2018.

"Flower Meanings & Symbolism." *FTD by Design*, www.ftd.com/blog/flower-meanings-and-symbolism. Accessed January 2018.

Gamma Phi Beta. Gamma Phi Beta Sorority, 2018, www.gammaphibeta.org. Accessed January 2018.

Giacobbe, Alyssa. "The Strange World of Sorority Rush Consultants." *Town and Country Magazine*, 15 Sept. 2017. www.townandcountrymag.com/leisure/arts-and-culture/a12108142/sorority-rush-consultants/. Accessed January 2018.

Glatter, Hayley. "The CEO's of Sorority Row." *The Atlantic*, 9 Sept. 2016, www.theatlantic.com/education/archive/2016/09/the-ceos-of-sorority-row/499331/. Accessed January 2018.

Goodman, Ruth. "The Quill of Alpha Xi Delta." *Serve in the Light of Truth: The Official Blog of Sigma Nu Fraternity*, 17 April 2015, sigmanublog.com/2015/04/17/sigma-nu-alpha-xi-deltas-alpha-males/. Accessed January 2018.

"History of Fraternity and Sorority Life in the US." *Elon University*. www.elon.edu/u/fraternity-and-sorority-life/about-us/history-of-fraternity-and-sorority-life-in-the-u-s/. Accessed January 2018.

"History at a Glance: Women in World War II." *The National World War II Museum: New Orleans*, www.nationalww2museum.org/students-teachers/student-resources/research-starters/women-wwii. Accessed January 2018.

"History of Greek Life." Appalachian State University, greeks.appstate.edu/history-of-greek-life. Accessed January 2018.

"History of the National Panhellenic Conference." *Valdosta State University*, www.valdosta.edu/student/student-life/greek-life/college-panhellenic-council/cpc-history.php. Accessed January 2018.

"History of the Women's Rights Movement." *National Women's History Project: Writing Women Back into History*, www.nwhp.org/resources/womens-rights-movement/history-of-the-womens-rights-movement/. Accessed January 2018.

Kappa Alpha Theta: Leading Women. Kappa Alpha Theta Fraternity, 1996-2018, www.kappaalphatheta.org. Accessed January 2018.

Kappa Delta Sorority: Building Confidence. Inspiring Action. Kappa Delta Sorority, www.kappadelta.org. Accessed January 2018.

Kappa Kappa Gamma: Aspire to Be. Kappa Kappa Gamma Fraternity, www.kappakappakappa.org. Accessed January 2018.

Kirby, Mandy and Vanessa Diffenbaugh. *A Victorian Flower Dictionary: The Language of Flowers Companion.* Ballantine Books, New York, 2011.

Lambert, Katie. "How Sororities Work." *How Stuff Works*, people.howstuffworks.com/sorority1.htm. Accessed January 2018.

"The Language of Flowers." *Smithsonian Gardens*, www.gardens.si.edu/come-learn/docs/Template_HistBloom_Language%20of%20Flowers.pdf. Accessed January 2018.

Lewis, Jone Johnson. "The History of Women in Higher Education." *Thought Co.*, 18 March 2017, www.thoughtco.com/history-women-higher-ed-4129738. Accessed January 2018.

"Manual of Information: 23rd Edition 2018." *National Panhellenic Conference*, January 2018, npcwomen.dynamic.omegafi.com/wp-content/uploads/sites/2037/2017/11/MOI-New-Brand-2017-cover.pdf. Accessed January 2018.

Martin, Ida Shaw. *The Sorority Handbook: Third Edition*. The Norburgh Press, 1909.

McNulty-Finn, Clara R. "Greek Life Timeline." *The Crimson*, 6 March 2014. www.thecrimson.com/article/2014/3/6/greek-life-timeline/. Accessed January 2018.

"The Meaning Behind Flower Colors." *Bloom Nation*, 26 July 2012, www.bloomnation.com/blog/the-meaning-behind-flower-colors/. Accessed January 2018.

Metzger, Mackenzie. "5 Things that Happen when you Become an Officer for Your Sorority." *Odyssey*, 14 Dec. 2015, www.theodysseyonline.com/five-things-that-happen-when-become-officer. Accessed January 2018.

Miller, Rachel Wilkerson and Terri Pous. "Here's What Sorority Recruitment is Really Like." *Buzzfeed*, 21 Sept. 2017, www.buzzfeed.com/terripous/the-no-bullshit-guide-to-sorority-rush?utm_term=.chLx3bV1DO#.cw9mvp65P4. Accessed January 2018.

Mongell, Susan and Alvin E. Roth. "Sorority Rush as a Two-Sided Matching Mechanism." *Department of Economics, University of Pittsburgh*, 31 Oct. 1996, www.pitt.edu/~daz1/sorority.html. Accessed January 2018.

Moore, Abigail Sullivan. "Pledge Prep." *The New York Times*, 16 July 2012, www.nytimes.com/2012/07/22/education/edlife/prepping-students-for-sorority-rush.html. Accessed January 2018.

"Nation's First Greek-Letter Sorority Founded in Greencastle." *DePauw University*, www.depauw.edu/news-media/latest-news/details/14026/. Accessed January 2018.

Norwood, Kendall. "What Sorority Initiation is Really Like." *Odyssey*, 13 Oct. 2015. www.theodysseyonline.com/what-sorority-initiation-really-is. Accessed January 2018.

NPC: National Panhellenic Conference. www.npcwomen.org/. Accessed January 2018.

"NPC Sorority Spotlight: 26 NPC Sororities Guide." *Sorority Sugar: Sweet on Greek*, sororitysugarhq.com/panhellenic/. Accessed January 2018.

"Our History." *Women's College Coalition*, www.womenscolleges.org/history. Accessed January 2018.

"Philanthropic History Inspires Our Cause." *Tales from Inside the Circle of Sisterhood*, 30 Jan. 2013, circleofsisterhoodfoundation.wordpress.com/2013/01/30/philanthropic-history-inspires-our-cause/. Accessed January 2018.

Pibetaphihq. "Holt House – Part 1." https://youtu.be/wYpo9MpqwY0. Online video clip. YouTube. YouTube, March 21, 2011. January 2018.

Phi Mu Fraternity: The Faithful Sisters. Phi Mu Fraternity, 2018, www.phimu.org. Accessed January 2018.

Phi Sigma Sigma: Once, Always. Phi Sigma Sigma Fraternity, 2015, www.phisigmasigma.org. Accessed January 2018.

Pi Beta Phi: Friends and Leaders for Life. Pi Beta Phi Fraternity, 2012, www.pibetaphi.org. Accessed January 2018.

Reilly, Lucas. "Why do Fraternities and Sororities have Greek Names?" *Mental Floss*, 1 Sept. 2015. mentalfloss.com/article/67988/why-do-fraternities-and-sororities-have-greek-names. Accessed January 2018.

Sigma Delta Tau: Empowering Women. Sigma Delta Tau Sorority, 2018. www.sigmadeltatau.org. Accessed January 2018.

Sigma Kappa: Live with Heart. Sigma Kappa Sorority, 2018, www.sigmakappa.org. Accessed January 2018.

Simpson, Amanda. "The Sorority and its Role in Women's Rights." *Medium*, 1 Dec. 2015, medium.com/@amandasimpson1851/the-sorority-and-its-role-in-women-s-rights-f1bdf2ecabd9. Accessed January 2018.

Stein, P.D. "Feminism and Sororities." *Odyssey*, 11 May 2016. www.theodysseyonline.com/feminism-sororities. Accessed January 2018.

Tanase, Nicolae. *The Language of Flowers.* Kindle Edition. Author. 2014-2017.

Theta Phi Alpha: Ever Loyal, Ever Lasting. Theta Phi Alpha Fraternity, 2018, thetaphialpha.org. Accessed January 2018.

Tri Delta. Delta Delta Delta Fraternity, 2018, www.tridelta.org. Accessed January 2018.

Tri Sigma: Empowered. Sigma Sigma Sigma Sorority, 2018, www.trisigma.org. Accessed January 2018.

Wade, Lisa. "Why Colleges Should Get Rid of Fraternities for Good." *Time*, 19, May 2017, time.com/4784875/fraternities-timothy-piazza/. Accessed January 2018.

Wells, Jonathon. "Is Man Up the Most Destructive Phrase in Modern Culture?" *The Telegraph*, 13 July 2015, www.telegraph.co.uk/men/thinking-man/11724215/Is-man -up-the-most-destructive-phrase-in-modern-culture.html. Accessed January 2018.

"What Happens at Fraternity and Sorority Initiation Ceremonies." *EduinReview*, eduin-review.com/blog/2010/08/what-happens-at-fraternity-and-sorority-initiation-ceremonies/. Accessed January 2018.

Winstead, J. Lloyd. *When Colleges Sang: The Story of Singing in American College Life.* University of Alabama Press. June 30, 2013.

"Women's Access to Higher Education: An Overview (1860-1948)." *HerStoria: History that Puts Woman in her Place*, 21 July 2012, herstoria.com/womens-access-to-higher-education-an-overview-1860-1948/. Accessed January 2018.

"Women During World War I." *Drawing America to Victory: The Persuasive Power of the Arts – An Online Exhibit by the Delaware Division of Historical and Cultural Affairs,* 2018, history.delaware.gov/exhibits/online/WWI/Women-roles-ww1.shtml#. Accessed January 2018.

"Women's Work in WWI." *Striking Women: Women and Work,* www.striking-women.org/ module/women-and-work/world-war-i-1914-1918. Accessed January 2018.

"Women in World War I." *The National Museum of American History,* americanhistory. si.edu/collections/object-groups/women-in-wwi. Accessed January 2018.

Zeta Tau Alpha: Seek the Noblest. Zeta Tau Alpha Fraternity, www.zetataualpha.org. Accessed January 2018.

Zimmer, Ben. "The Meaning of Man Up." *The New York Times Magazine*, 3 Sept. 2010. www.nytimes.com/2010/09/05/magazine/05FOB-onlanguage-t.html. Accessed January 2018.